STIR

Share Your Thoughts

With the Author: Your comments will be forwarded to the author when you send them to *zauthor@zondervan.com*.

With Zondervan: Submit your review of this book by writing to *zreview@zondervan.com*.

Free Online Resources at
www.zondervan.com

Daily Bible Verses and Devotions: Enrich your life with daily Bible verses or devotions that help you start every morning focused on God. Visit www.zondervan.com/newsletters.

Free Email Publications: Sign up for newsletters on Christian living, academic resources, church ministry, fiction, children's resources, and more. Visit www.zondervan.com/newsletters.

Zondervan Bible Search: Find and compare Bible passages in a variety of translations at www.zondervanbiblesearch.com.

Other Benefits: Register to receive online benefits like coupons and special offers, or to participate in research.

STIR

SPIRITUAL TRANSFORMATION IN RELATIONSHIPS

Mindy Caliguire

ZONDERVAN®
.com

WILLOW CREEK
ASSOCIATION

ZONDERVAN

STIR
Copyright © 2013 by Mindy Caliguire

This title is also available as a Zondervan ebook. Visit www.zondervan.com/ebooks.

Requests for information should be addressed to:
Zondervan, *Grand Rapids, Michigan 49530*

Library of Congress Cataloging-in-Publication Data

Caliguire, Mindy, 1965-.
    STIR : spiritual transformation in relationships / Mindy Caliguire.
      pages cm
    ISBN 978-0-310-49482-9 (pbk.)
     1. Spiritual formation. 2. Discipling (Christianity) 3. Interpersonal relations—
Religious aspects—Christianity. 4. Small groups—Religious aspects—Christianity.
I. Title.
BV4511.C255 2013
253.5'3—dc23
                                         2013009226

Cover design and illustration: John Hamilton Design
Interior design: David Conn, Ben Fetterley

Printed in the United States of America

13 14 15 16 17 18 /DCI/ 20 19 18 17 16 15 14 13 12 11 10 9 8 7 6 5 4 3 2 1

To my husband, Jeff,
and our sons—Jeffrey, Jonathan, and Joshua—
who model radical inclusivity
and create purposeful community
everywhere they go

CONTENTS

FOREWORD

It is very hard to take care of something if you don't know how it works. Not being the mechanical type, I have been responsible for the deterioration of everything from furnaces to lawn mowers to cars, based on that one simple principle.

We are bombarded every day by messages about caring for all the parts of our bodies. Diet books routinely dominate the "how-to" bestseller lists; exercise videos range from "gentle care" to "outrageously insane" in their intensity of focus; doctors regularly get inundated with prescription recommendations from patients who hear about some medication from an infomercial or Katie or Oprah or Dr. Oz.

Then there is the soul.

If it's hard to care for something you don't understand, it's even harder to care for something you're not sure exists. We live in a society that has perhaps never paid more attention to our outer being and never paid less to our inner being. But the soul will not go away. If it is neglected or abused or ill-treated or overwhelmed, it is life in its wholeness and fullness that gets shattered.

This is the condition that Mindy Caliguire seeks to remedy. She writes as one who cares deeply about the soul. She has not just read and thought about it; she has been actively engaged on the front lines of church ministry to seek to discover how real people can learn deep wisdom and bring healing and vitality to the fractures and fissures of their minds and hearts and wills. She also writes as a wife and a mom who seeks this learning in the middle of all the fullness of family life and contemporary demands.

The soul, although full of mystery, is not meant to be confusing. It can be damaged by forces we all understand—ignorance, falsehood, pain, and—above all—sin. It can be healed only by a power greater than ourselves, but that does not mean we are passive. The Bible is filled with descriptions of the means of grace by which our souls can be restored. Deep fellowship with other people, habit-altering times of solitude and silence, acts of generosity and days of servanthood, and lives of simplicity and celebrations of joy are all described here in a way that is accessible and winsome and magnetic.

"The law of the LORD is perfect, refreshing the soul," wrote the psalmist many centuries ago (Psalm 19:7). That does not mean legalism refreshes the soul. But it does mean that understanding how God created life to work can be the beginning of hope. When that understanding begins to be applied, when we respond in faith by actually offering our time and our bodies and our thoughts for renewal, we are surprised to find that we meet Another. We step into a reality where our souls can be cared for from beyond ourselves. Jesus is there. And the soul finds its worth.

May the reading of this book be a journey to the center of your soul, and then a journey infinitely greater than that to the Maker and Redeemer and Lover of your soul.

— John Ortberg

PREFACE
A SOLITARY JOURNEY

Among the first things I did to launch my ministry, Soul Care, was to exhibit a new line of prayer journals at the annual must-attend event for Christian retailers—the Christian Booksellers Association convention. This event, I was told, was *the* place to make my debut.

With an existing customer base of ten independent bookstores and the boundless enthusiasm of a new entrepreneur, I signed up for the event well in advance, eager to prove I was really serious about this. A few months later, I packed my bags and quirky display and headed to the big time—the ten-thousand-square-foot convention center in Orlando, Florida. I knew this was an important step, and I couldn't wait to see what God might have for me.

I was so excited the first day of the convention that I arrived at the earliest possible time to begin setting up my eight-by-eight-foot booth. In comparison to the palatial booths of most of the other exhibitors, my booth might better have been called a hovel. But it was mine, and I was determined to make the best of it.

As I set up my 0.0008 of the exhibit hall, I discovered yet another indication that I didn't quite belong—and perhaps it was an indication that my Soul Care vision might be easily misunderstood. The conference organizers provided a sign for my booth—a slim, nondescript white rectangle with ten-inch black letters that read "Sole Care."

SOLE CARE

Needless to say, I took down the sign. I wasn't planning on using it anyway. But it made me think about the employees of convention centers who walk on those concrete floors every day, all year long. My feet are sore after just a few days! Maybe all they can think about is the "sole" of their foot.

But I found another deep irony in the misnomer as well. You see, for many Christ followers, the "Christian life," our journey with God on this earth, is a "sole"—as in *solo*—experience. Even when we are surrounded by family and friends and gather together at well-attended churches, we too often walk the journey of faith *alone*.

Sadly, we are accustomed to "sole" care.

NOT THE WAY IT'S SUPPOSED TO BE*

Have you ever felt that way about your faith—that it's just a you-and-God thing? We know that life with God is supposed to involve loving people and being involved in community. But really, who has time for all that fluffy stuff? And why bother when it often seems to result in disappointment at best and a heap of frustration and trouble at worst?

It doesn't have to be this way. Not only is this individualistic pattern of spiritual life something early church leaders never intended; it's safe to say they would have found it unimaginable. Consider this description of what was *normal* for the first generation of Christ followers:

---

* Borrowed from the title of Cornelius Plantinga's book, *Not the Way It's Supposed to Be* (Grand Rapids: Eerdmans, 1995).

They devoted themselves to the apostles' teaching and to fellowship, to the breaking of bread and to prayer. Everyone was filled with awe at the many wonders and signs performed by the apostles. All the believers were together and had everything in common. They sold property and possessions to give to anyone who had need. Every day they continued to meet together in the temple courts. They broke bread in their homes and ate together with glad and sincere hearts, praising God and enjoying the favor of all the people. And the Lord added to their number daily those who were being saved.

— Acts 2:42 – 47

The relationships that marked this community were a reflection of the deep transformation they had experienced as individuals. By God's design, relationships in this new community increasingly *defined* them as they laid aside cultural and religious affiliations. In addition, these new relationships *produced* in them the *character formation* that would identify them as Jesus' own people — his unique community.

I believe many Christians today head in a dangerous direction when they neglect these essential relationships and decide they can do without a community that enfolds and nurtures the life of God within them. While some long to have deep, transformational relationships, they may have been wounded in the past and are now distrustful. I've been on both sides of the wounding, and it is sad and tragic. But isolation is not the solution to our pain. Whatever the cause, whatever pain has wounded us or hurt us, isolating ourselves from the community of Jesus' followers can kill off the life of God in us.

For most people today, church is no longer seen as a community of relationships; instead, the church is seen as an institution, a selection of services offered by a set of religious professionals. If you can find one that meets your needs, you'll be set. Perhaps this consumeristic view explains why so many feel like they have stalled in their relationship with God — "These services just don't do anything for me." This may also explain why the people of God do not consistently convey the character, or likeness, of God. If we treat the church as a place where we are served, we rarely give anything back and consequently never grow. Professional religious leaders can't do our spiritual growth for us.

In Scripture, Jesus' people were thought of as a community called the *ecclesia*—the "called-out" ones. Invisible spiritual bonds connected them to one another—bonds significant to their ongoing spiritual life and growth. The metaphor that best describes this depth of connection is a human body—having distinct members, being interconnected and interdependent. Purposeful work, maturation, and healing occur in the context of a unified, deeply connected whole. Relational isolation just doesn't fit with the way the church as a God-infused, God-centered community was designed to exist. But there is good news. God's vision for community—the church as the body of Christ—can be restored and renewed. And it can have dramatic implications, releasing the church to engage in the work of God, living as the people of God.

TRANSFORMATION IN THE CHURCH

REVEAL is an extensive and ongoing spiritual life research study initiated in 2007 by the Willow Creek Association.[1] As church leaders studied the research and wrestled with its implications, many of them wondered what they should do. I've worked with many of these leaders to develop spiritual formation strategies for their ministries, and three questions invariably come up:

1. How do we migrate from one-size-fits-all small groups to something more effective for people at all stages of spiritual growth?
2. How do we best teach spiritual practices?
3. How do we motivate mature believers to keep growing?

These are important questions, and the way we answer these questions can greatly affect the spiritual growth of the people in our churches. Let's look at each of these questions separately.

A Vision for Small Groups

Most leaders have discovered, through trial and error, that a one-size-fits-all approach to small group ministry does not work. In other words, pastors and church leaders should no longer expect that simply having a small group program in place will lead to transformational relationships for everyone in their church. In fairness, this may have never been the stated goal of small group ministry, but over time it has become the default assumption. If you ask a pastor how people grow and develop in their church, they are most likely to point you to their small group program.

Sadly, those programs don't always lead to transformed people.

One church leader shared, "The vast majority of our adults are actively involved in small groups, so we assumed discipleship was happening. But lately we're not so sure." Though many faithfully attend the church's small groups, leaders don't observe much evidence of transformation in individual lives. They fear their vision for "life on life" discipleship through small groups has become, in their words, merely "life on curriculum."

Small groups have a place. They can be vitally important for growth, particularly in the early stages of the spiritual journey. But they can also become stifling or even harmful to ongoing growth and spiritual development if they fail to change. Shifts in both form and function that release people into new relational environments are needed. As people grow, they need relationships that fit their particular stage of growth.

This book will help you better understand the types of relationships that are needed at different stages of spiritual growth. My goal is to show how different kinds of relationships can facilitate growth, whether those relationships call themselves small groups, spiritual friendships, or something else altogether. What matters is not the particular name or form of the relationship, but that there are ongoing relational connections that meet each person in a way that is appropriate to the way God is working in them, changing and transforming them into Christlikeness. Life change happens in relationships, but it doesn't always happen in small groups.

Teaching Spiritual Practices

Many churches offer dozens of weekly Bible studies and education classes, yet these churches still desire to help people grow as disciples. How might they help people actually learn how to pray? Are there opportunities to learn from another follower of Christ how to practice spiritual disciplines? These spiritual practices are vitally important to the process of transformation. They expand our ability to notice and respond to God's deeply personal involvement in our daily lives. They help us give God access to the deepest, most broken parts of our lives. But how does a church teach and train a person in these spiritual practices? How might a church incorporate this learning as a normal part of their congregational life? These questions are challenging to answer, and many churches are eager to come up with models that work.

Sometimes churches will begin by hiring a spiritual formation pastor. But then the question becomes: What does this person do? I consulted with one associate pastor who returned from an extended medical leave only to discover that he was now the spiritual formation pastor. He had no specific idea what that meant, nor did those who had changed his job title in his absence!

Even when senior leaders are well acquainted with spiritual formation and are determined to teach others, they find very few in their congregation who seem interested in learning. One senior pastor shared how after a season of spiritual dryness he was finding new rhythms of spiritual practices that were creating a whole new space for God in his life. But week after lonely week, he met with a wall of resistance when he stood behind the pulpit to preach. He would invite others to these deeper places but received little response. Why? He realized that his people wanted a simple, clear, practical message about God — three points and an illustration — in under thirty minutes. It was the "formula" they were accustomed to getting. So how could he awaken them to the deeper life of the soul? How could he challenge them to take steps to develop their own life with God rather than having it spoon-fed to them each week? Like many pastors, he wants to help his people move beyond knowledge about God toward an inner journey with God, but to do so will require changing what they have come to think of as "normal" in their experience of church — and of God.

The good news is that with clear vision, strong teaching, and the right relational environments, it is possible to *normalize* this process of learning the core spiritual practices, making it a routine aspect of the life of the church.

Challenging Mature Believers

Relationships are not just for new or young believers. Mature believers also need relationships for their ongoing spiritual growth, and they need them in two important ways. Not surprisingly, mature believers grow spiritually when they are assisting or mentoring others. Yet, as important as investment in others is, mature believers also need relational environments in which they are *not* leading, relationships in which they are being personally challenged. Sometimes churches inadvertently compromise these peer-to-peer relationships by emphasizing the importance of the investments these folks make in others — but this can have consequences. It may lead mature believers to burn out or stall in their own spiritual growth. To counter this, churches need to understand the unique needs of mature believers and continue to assist and shepherd them in their ongoing spiritual journey.

We will look at these unique needs in later sections of this book as we invite church leaders to consider the importance of transformational relationships at all stages of the Christian spiritual journey. These relationships can and must change as people mature. If we design our discipleship and spiritual formation process with this in mind, we are likely to see greater levels of authentic transformation happening in and through the local church. But this requires some fundamental shifts out of our isolation and into intentional, meaningful relationships that are focused Godward.

SOUL CARE AS CARE OF SOULS

For much of my own journey, I considered soul care as things I do to care for my own soul — the classic spiritual practices or disciplines that, in turn, open me up to the care of God. I often think of soul care as something I do for myself, as an individual. And while that idea has been helpful, the traditional use of this phrase as it dates back to the ancient church is relationally focused. Historically, soul care is the care we give to the souls of *others*, not ourselves.

Gary Moon and David Benner, visionary leaders in contemporary Christian soul care, provide a helpful background on the origin of this phrase:

> The English phrase "care of souls" has its origins in the Latin *cura animarum*. While *cura* is most commonly translated "care," it actually contains the idea of both care and cure. *Care* refers to actions designed to support the well-being of something or someone. *Cure* refers to actions designed to restore well-being that has been lost. The Christian church has historically embraced both meanings of *cura* and has understood soul care to involve nurture and support as well as healing and restoration.[2]

The goal of this book is to present a new vision for this dimension of soul care—learning how to care for the spiritual growth and well-being of people at every stage of the journey through God-centered, spiritually challenging relationships. If the powerful potential for soul care and soul cure can be seen as a rocket poised to launch but still sitting on the launchpad, let's begin by looking at the fuel: Holy Spirit–infused relationships. To begin the transition from a pseudo-community of aching isolation—*sole care*—to a community that truly cares for souls, we need to begin with a biblical vision for spiritual growth in the context of relationships.

INTRODUCTION
ROCKET FUEL FOR THE SOUL

RUNNING TOGETHER

The first book I ever wanted to write some fifteen years ago was on the topic of relationships that help us mature and grow. I wanted to call it *Running Together*. Why *Running Together*? I found I could easily relate to the words of the author of Hebrews:

> Therefore, since we are surrounded by such a great cloud of witnesses, let us throw off everything that hinders and the sin that so easily entangles. And let us run with perseverance the race marked out for us, fixing our eyes on Jesus, the pioneer and perfecter of faith. For the joy set before him he endured the cross, scorning its shame, and sat down at the right hand of the throne of God. Consider him who endured such opposition from sinners, so that you will not grow weary and lose heart.
>
> — Hebrews 12:1–3

The good news was that I wasn't running alone. God was using an unexpected assortment of unique and intentional relationships to change things within me and around me. Through these new relationships, each of us was learning how to run the various races marked out for us. We were running in different ways, but we were running together.

Who ran with me? This unexpected assortment of unique relationships began to include some of the people who had been in a "small group" I led. It included some spiritual directors, friends who had been in twelve-step recovery groups, and some mentors who later became friends. These relationships ebbed and flowed naturally and did not always overlap with each other.

Over time, these spiritual companions and I learned the unique races that God had marked out for each of us. Together, we threw off the things that hindered our progress. Together, we abandoned sin that so easily entangled us. Together, we learned to endure. Together, we fixed our eyes on Jesus. And together, we were transformed — set free and released to serve, lead, impact, and bless others. We discovered the rocket fuel for our souls — the power of God to help us run, grow, change, and persevere in following Jesus.

What made this so unusual is the fact that I preferred — if left to myself — to run alone. If it hadn't been for deep pain and some gracious wounded healers, I never would have learned to invite these relationships into my life. I never would have learned to trust others to be used by God to help me grow.

RUNNING AWAY

In college, I remember thinking it would be ideal if I could follow Jesus by living alone in a remote shack in the mountains of Montana. I wanted to live as far away as possible from the complexity and pain of relationships. Left to myself, I might have ended up there, living in the woods by myself. But my gregarious, ministry-minded husband had other ideas — and they eventually led us to an internship at Willow Creek Community Church in the early 1990s.

One of the first assignments we received in our leadership development process was to read Dr. Henry Cloud's book, *When Your*

World Makes No Sense (now available under the title *Changes That Heal*). Prior to reading, though, we were given an assessment. Sitting in my office overlooking the parking lot at Willow Creek, I answered the questions for just the first portion of the book, and then, proud of my answers, I tallied my score.

Like many similar tests, the questions corresponded to numerical scores, which are then grouped and labeled to help you diagnose where you are on the spectrum. As it turned out, the first section of *When Your World Makes No Sense* dealt with the topic of bonding with others.

I had a very low score, and I soon realized that the highest values represented "strong bonding," and slightly lower scores were still "healthy levels of bonding." Much lower scores were labeled "at-risk levels of bonding."

I scored in the "May not have a pulse" level of bonding.*

In other words, I failed miserably. But worst of all was the fact that I had been confident I was answering the questions *correctly*! This was a wake-up call, showing me how flawed and misguided my thinking was. Reading the book confirmed that in order to truly become whole and mature, I needed to greatly increase my capacity to bond with others. I had to unlearn a lifetime of poor bonding with others—and even with God.

Several months later, at my mid-year evaluation, I received this feedback from my internship supervisors: "We see that you're really strong in project managing, involving others, and casting vision. We feel confident you can effectively handle anything we ask you to do with excellence. But we do have one question, and we are very concerned about your answer: Who is taking care of Mindy?"

I sat in silence for what seemed like a long time. I was prepared to be asked just about anything—except that question. I willed myself not to shed tears, but I knew that just saying "God" wasn't going to cut it. I was performing well. But I was running alone. Dangerously alone.

Thankfully, my season of running *away* from relationships was about to end.

---

* I don't think this was exactly the wording for this category, but it sums up my score quite nicely.

RUNNING IN COMMUNITY

I'll share more about my own journey and the things I've learned about transitioning from "sole" care to authentic, life-giving relationships with others in the body of Christ in the chapters to come. Relationships with other believers have profoundly shaped me into the person I am today. Small group members, spiritual friends, and mentors have spurred me on to pursue God and walk in faith.

Now, as I work in this area of spiritual formation with churches and their leaders, I've had a growing concern that deep relationships are unusual. As we talk about discipleship and spiritual formation, I notice that a focus on fostering a variety of relationships for the intentional purpose of spiritual growth seems to be weak and in some cases is entirely absent.

As a result, many people today are on a solo journey with God, even if they attend a church. Rarely do people in churches see intentional relationships as a vital component of their spiritual growth. Many know it's important to grow in knowledge and understanding—studying the Bible, learning basic Christian beliefs—and this is good and necessary. The book of Hebrews has much to say about this as well: "Therefore let us move beyond the elementary teachings about Christ and be taken forward to maturity, not laying again the foundation of repentance from acts that lead to death, and of faith in God …" (Hebrews 6:1).

But as important as it is to grow in our individual knowledge of the Bible and the teachings of the Christian faith, our quest for growth and maturity must take place in community. Accountable, encouraging, and intentional relationships with other believers should be a normative part of our experience as Christians—and it can be if we're leading others toward full transformation in the context of the church. Again, the writer of Hebrews brings both the challenge of deepening spiritual growth and the challenge that we belong to a meaningful community:

> Therefore, brothers and sisters, since we have confidence to enter the Most Holy Place by the blood of Jesus, by a new and living way opened for us through the curtain, that is,

his body, and since we have a great priest over the house of God, *let us draw near to God* with a sincere heart and with the full assurance that faith brings, having our hearts sprinkled to cleanse us from a guilty conscience and having our bodies washed with pure water. *Let us hold unswervingly to the hope we profess*, for he who promised is faithful. *And let us consider how we may spur one another on toward love and good deeds*, not giving up meeting together, as some are in the habit of doing, but encouraging one another—and all the more as you see the Day approaching.

— Hebrews 10:19–25, emphasis added

Christian community is founded on the work of Jesus. His sacrifice is the basis for our new life, our inclusion in the people of God. Yet this is not something that only affects us as individuals. To grow in our faith, we come together as a community.

So how do we see this vision become reality? How do we recover the vital place of relationships in the process of spiritual growth—at *all* stages of spiritual growth? We need a new way of looking at our growth, recognizing that there are distinct stages in the journey of faith and understanding that the types of relationships at each stage are different and unique. In the chapters that follow, I will introduce you to a framework that has been helpful to pastors and church leaders as they wrestle with these questions, and I will also flesh out this framework in greater detail, noting the ministry implications where relevant.

We'll discover key developmental markers for three distinct stages in the spiritual journey and explore the kinds of relationships that are most conducive to spiritual growth in each stage. Hopefully you'll agree that when working right, these relationships can be rocket fuel for the soul.

THE THREE STAGES

The three stages of spiritual growth and formation are Learning Together, Journeying Together, and Following Together. You may notice that these stages bear a strong likeness to the three "believer" segments highlighted by the REVEAL study: Growing in Christ, Close to Christ, and Christ-Centered. The labels used in this book reflect the unique developmental dynamics of the formation process, and I've added the term *together* as a reminder that these developments happen best in relationship.

Three primary "moves" between spiritual growth stages have been identified through the REVEAL research and were highlighted in the book titled *Move*. These are the primary shifts that mark transition from one stage of growth to another.[1]

> First "Move": Core Beliefs
> Second "Move": Spiritual Practices
> Third "Move": Giving Away Your Life

In addition to the developmental work needed within each stage, I will be looking at two essential *relational* elements that are necessary for each stage of development: *Direction* and *Discernment*. As we'll see, the relationship between these elements changes over time.

Direction refers to the level of structure in a relationship—how much instruction and guidance are needed to support growth. In a highly directive relationship, strong, clear leadership is offered. Often, a formal curriculum or plan supports the process.

On the other hand, as one grows, the need for relationships that offer *discernment* grows as well. Discernment refers to a more complex level of interaction where a person helps another by offering observations and wisdom in such a way that an individual is enabled to wisely make decisions without explicit direction or counsel. So, for example, while a job-training seminar provides a highly directive environment for learning new work skills, in contrast, a manager best helps an employee improve and grow through his or her discernment—offering specific insight and guidance as the work progresses.

Spiritual Transformation in Relationships

| Stage 1: | Stage 2: | Stage 3: |
| Learning Together | Journeying Together | Following Together |

Both of the relational gifts of direction and discernment remain important throughout the spiritual journey. But their relative importance shifts as people mature, with the need for discernment increasing as the need for direction decreases. New believers in the Learning Together stage need high levels of direction in their relationships and clear guidance from their leaders or spiritual mentors. How can they learn the basics of the Christian faith without strong, clear direction? How will they learn the discipline of prayer unless someone models it for them, walking them through the practice in detailed steps?

For those farther along in the journey, the need for strong direction *decreases*. Often, these believers don't need or want a curriculum to teach them about the Bible or detailed steps outlining a program for how to walk with God. They've learned the basics and know how to find whatever else they need. At this stage, it's less about the how-to and more about discovering, "Where is God at work right now, and how can I join him?"

The three stages are listed below with their corresponding developmental objective and ideal relational style.

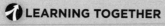 **LEARNING TOGETHER**

Objective: Establish core beliefs, biblical literacy, and the fundamentals of a relationship with God

Kind of relationship: Highly directive

⊘ JOURNEYING TOGETHER

Objective: Develop familiarity with one's story, acknowledge brokenness, and cultivate increasing dependence on God through spiritual practices

Kind of relationship: Nearly equal amounts of direction and discernment

⊘ FOLLOWING TOGETHER

Objective: Build an increasingly discerning life on a solid foundation of biblical knowledge and a strong relationship with God

Kind of relationship: Highly discerning and minimally directive

The Learning Together section of *STIR* (part 1: chapters 1–2) highlights the important growth that happens through relationships early in our spiritual development. In Journeying Together (part 2: chapters 3–4), I'll explore the dynamics of relationships that can help us face the interior journey, finding God and deep transformation as we look within—with the help of other people. Because many churches don't plan for or support this stage of growth, maturing believers tend to look outside the community of their local church; at worst, they become disillusioned and forgo church altogether. Instead of abandoning those who enter the Journeying Together stage, we can develop a plan to receive those in this stage and include their experience in the vision for spiritual formation. The final stage of the spiritual formation process, Following Together (part 3: chapters 5–6), describes the kinds of relationships that keep us at full stride in the race marked out for us as we serve others in love and commit for the long haul, persevering until the end.

Interestingly, the REVEAL research confirms a shift in the kinds of relationships that support spiritual development in more mature believers. Cally Parkinson, coauthor of *Move*, writes, "Spiritual community shows up as a growth catalyst in all three [spiritual growth]

movements, though the specific form of that community shifts as people grow in faith from more casual friendships to mentor relationships, relationships that typically involve greater accountability and intimacy."[2]

So the church as *ecclesia* plays an essential role in all of these spiritual growth stages, but the way in which the church engages with people—through organized activities like weekend services and small groups, for example—shifts as people spiritually mature. Cally Parkinson explains:

> Our research suggests that it's very important for churches to encourage formal, organized gatherings—like small groups and serving experiences—but it's also okay for people to let go of the organized structure at some point. A key output of the organized structure is to allow powerful informal relational networks to develop, which implies that the role of the organized structure may be temporary.[3]

We experience spiritual growth in the context of community through *different* people at *different* stages of our spiritual journey, bearing in mind that it is ultimately God who brings about spiritual growth, not a program or another person or relationship. The apostle Paul writes in 1 Corinthians 3:6, "I planted the seed, Apollos watered it, but God has been making it grow."

At the end of each chapter you will find a section called "What's Stirring?" I encourage you to set aside time to reflect on the questions included there and to think about your own spiritual journey. On occasion, I've also included questions for leaders to ask as they serve others on their path.

LEARNING FROM THOSE IN MINISTRY

Before I conclude this introduction, I want to introduce you to two of my friends in ministry—Barb and Emily. These friends serve the local church in two very different settings, and their stories are helpful as we begin to look at the importance of relationships in our spiritual growth and development. Let's begin with Barb.

Barb's Story

My friend Barb Roose serves as directional leader/pastor of spiritual formation at CedarCreek Church, a dynamic, growing, multisite, highly evangelistic church near Toledo. Recently, I met her at a local Starbucks to talk about her ministry and her passion for transformation. On a brown napkin, we worked out the general outlines of the framework discussed in this book. Here, I've asked Barb to share how some of these ideas have practically impacted her own ministry context in Toledo:

I realized it was possible—actually necessary—to shift our group leader training model from "set it and forget it," where one size and one kind of training fit all, to a "life cycle" leadership model, where we expect and even plan for changes in groups, and in leaders, as they mature.

Through the use of this simple idea, I found a new way to cast vision to our leaders about expecting a life cycle for their leadership. It also provided an easy-to-convey format I could communicate to my pastoral leadership team.

I also began to dream. First, I visualized an initial group of leaders who were ready to jump-start a new believer's walk by teaching through structured curriculum and "parenting" the early development of the new believer. Then I saw those group leaders handing off that new believer to the next group leader, whose gifting was in being able to manage those "middle years"—that crucial time period when growing believers have just enough information to be dangerous, but they're not yet mature. Finally, I visualized a set of group leaders available to receive the maturing believer. These leaders appreciate the watering and tilling efforts of the previous group leaders and relish the opportunity to walk beside the maturing believer in a mentoring relationship that has very little instruction but high discernment.

I took the brown napkin home as a memento of our

discussion and used it to share this concept with my senior pastor and campus pastors a few weeks later. I watched as they tilted their heads in interest at this new way of equipping our precious group leaders. This has been an exciting new path to explore as a ministry leader, and I look forward to bringing our group leaders along for the journey down this new road.

Though Barb's specific points of application will differ from your own context and ministry application, hopefully they begin to give you a sense of how this simple shift in thinking about the relational dimension of spiritual growth and formation can inform your strategy for ministry. These changes will help Barb to both facilitate growth in the people of her community at *all* stages of spiritual development and support the leaders who will guide others in their development. Instead of adopting a one-size-fits-all approach, she can now focus on connecting people in relationships with one another, helping them meet folks who have a similar maturity in the faith. Barb is also excited to have a new way of honoring the relationships that mature believers have developed, helping them "stay in the game" and continue growing and maturing, while also challenging them to serve as mentors and guides to others.

Emily's Story

My friend Emily has also been impacted by this framework for spiritual growth in relationships. Her story, by contrast, is quite humorous—and disconcerting! It shows what can happen when we don't have adequate vision for each stage of the journey.

Emily serves on staff at National Community Church in Washington DC. Her supervisor, Heather Zempel, oversees the discipleship of new believers and the spiritual growth of members at the church. I met Emily when she traveled with Heather to Chicago for a speaking engagement. Under some welcome shade from the hot summer sunshine, we sat at patio tables near my office and spoke of our deep passion for transformation and discipleship in the local church. Heather urged Emily to share the details of her first venture into church leadership.

We laughed as she shared her story, but it was laughter punctuated with a certain amount of pain.

As I was growing up, my church experience was quite limited and never personally meaningful. But during my freshman year of college, I decided to pursue a faith of my own. I hadn't darkened the door of a church in years.

One thing I knew about Christians in the South (where I lived)—they loved to highlight their Bibles. So the night before going to church, I took out a brand-new Bible and some highlighters. Randomly, I started highlighting the text throughout, making it look like I had read it cover to cover. I varied the colors so it wouldn't look like I had highlighted it all in one sitting. After all, the better the Christian, the more vibrant the Bible.

A few months after this "highlighting" incident, I was recruited to be a new small group leader. Unfortunately, no one ever stopped to ask me if I was ready to lead. While I have natural leadership gifts, there were some gaping holes in my personal discipleship. But no one knew; no one asked. Amazingly, my role of leading a small group quickly turned into an internship and then a full-time staff position at a large church. After a year of doing this, I began to realize that my character—and what I knew of God's character—wasn't keeping pace with my level of influence. I faced the truth: I was more committed to Christian culture than I was to God.

I took a step down and a step back. I joined the Protégé Program at National Community Church with Heather. During my year as a protégé, I found I could still operate out of my gift set and grow as a leader. But far more important than my ability to lead was the growth in my character. That happened through transformational relationships.

It can be good to highlight verses in your Bible, but it's easy

to fill your Bible with these highlights and never change. I've
learned that spiritual growth is more about the verses that God
highlights on my heart than about what I've highlighted in my
Bible. Following Jesus isn't about fitting into the crowd, but
about fitting my life into his. It's not about my performance; it's
about his presence.

Both Barb and Emily illustrate why we need a developmental, flexible framework for spiritual growth in the church. Barb's leaders now have a long-term vision for their own growth, as well as for the growth of those they serve. Emily has come to realize that being gifted, talented, and capable doesn't always equate to life change and maturity. She has come to recognize her own need for relationships that see her for who she really is and not as just another person to fill an open position in a program.

I pray that the journey we take through the pages of this book will open the door to practical ideas and changes you can make to support the growth of your community through intentional relationships.

We'll begin at the beginning — the Learning Together stage — and see how we can best support those in this stage.

WHAT'S STIRRING?

1. Write out the four directives given in Hebrews 12:1 – 3.
    What expression do they currently have in your life, if
    any? Which one seems the most confusing or challeng-
    ing to you today? Why?

2. Who are you "running together" with right now? Who
    has run with you in the past?

3. Think of those you currently lead in your church. Which
    stage of the framework do you see each person as
    occupying — Learning Together, Journeying Together, or
    Following Together?

PART 1

LEARNING TOGETHER

CHAPTER 1
START STRONG

One of the first Bible study groups I ever attended was at the Sigma Chi fraternity house at Cornell University. We were a hodge-podge of academics, sorority girls, fraternity boys, star athletes, mature believers (there must have been at least one), nonbelievers, and quasi-believers. I'll put myself in that last category.

The lacrosse player who introduced me to the group was a guy named Frank. Some time later, Frank shared with me his first experience with the group. He had never attended a Bible study before, so he entered the second-story room sheepishly, and after surveying the one or two available seats in the room, he wormed his way between the three pretty coeds already squished together on the couch.

The leader opened in prayer and instructed the group to turn to Ephesians 2 so they could read it together. Frank panicked. He had no idea where Ephesians was, or even *what* Ephesians was. So he turned to the woman next to him and coolly asked, "Where's Ephesians?" She replied, "Next to Galatians." *Great.* As if he knew where Galatians was! Frank was in desperate need of some *direction*.

He had no idea where to start, and he needed someone to come alongside and help him understand.

Perhaps you've been in a situation similar to Frank's, where everyone but you seemed to know the drill. Or maybe you've led groups where the people attending know absolutely nothing about the Bible or its doctrines. I once led a group where one of the people attending, a woman named Anne, had once believed that the Trinity was Jesus, Mary, and Joseph (a phrase often used as an expletive in some parts of the country!). She learned this basic and vital Christian doctrine before coming to the group, but the point is we all need to internalize these foundational ideas.

Frank and Anne represent some of the unique needs of those who are entering the "on-ramp" of spiritual development. They are in a growing relationship with God, but they are learning how to merge their modern, secular lives with the great historic and present-day stream of God's activity among his people. There is a lot of excitement, but plenty of confusion as well. And much room to grow.

As with newbies in any endeavor, there are many new things for them to learn, and one of the most powerful ways they'll learn is through relationships with other believers. *Learning* is what defines this stage—that's why we call it the Learning Together stage (creative, I know). Because of the vast amount of learning that takes place in this stage, a highly directive relationship is needed, one that allows growth to happen in a focused and logical manner.

Though it's been several years since I first learned some of these foundational spiritual truths, I can certainly relate to the feelings of confusion that people have when they are learning something new. A rather silly analogy, but still quite real, is in the realm of learning to play video games. My sons tell me I am a "n00b"—someone who knows nothing. Truth be told, if I'm ever going to learn a video game, it will only happen if they take the time to teach me every little detail. (I finally learned LittleBigPlanet, but even with their help I never could get the hang of Super Mario Bros.) When I play a video game, there is just so much to look at, so much activity, that it leaves me utterly confused. It's a whole new world, completely unfamiliar. I don't understand the rules, the dangers, or even, sometimes, the point. It's "game over" before I've even begun.

The spiritual life can look just as bewildering to someone who is absorbing a new set of beliefs, growing in a relationship with an unseen Being, developing new friendships, and learning the Scriptures—often for the first time in their lives. For some new believers, it's "game over" just as they are getting started. You see, without a proper foundation in the basic beliefs and practices of the faith, these new disciples of Christ are vulnerable. It takes commitment and deliberate focus to walk with them developmentally to the point when they mature in their relationship with God and grow in their faith. It's far easier to simply allow them to become absorbed into the Christian subculture of the church. But that doesn't mean they are growing. A person can attend church and even be involved in leadership and yet never take steps to

"Disciples of Jesus are those who are with him learning to be like him. That is, they are learning to lead their life, their actual existence, as he would lead their life if he were they. This is what they are learning together in their local gatherings, and with those gatherings a constant part of their life, they are learning how to walk with Jesus and learn from him in every aspect of their individual lives."

Dallas Willard,
Renovation of the Heart

grow and mature in their faith. They can be a cultural Christian, but not a growing disciple.

If growth is to occur, significant progress must be made in helping these new believers grasp the core beliefs of the faith, understand the Scriptures, and gain comprehension that extends beyond mere head knowledge. Growing and maturing followers of Christ will begin to see themselves as part of the bigger picture of God's greater story. The progress they make through the Learning Together stage sets them up for a lifetime of following God.

LEARNING TO DRIVE IN BOSTON

One night at small group, Lisa suddenly and unexpectedly blurted out, "I get it!" We looked at her, wondering what she meant. During this particular study, we were exploring how various themes are carried out through the Scriptures. Lisa went on to explain: "Since first becoming a Christian, I have been learning about the Bible and its importance in my life. But through our group, I've begun to see the Bible differently. Now I get it! This is the same thing that happened when I was learning to drive in Boston."

Now *we* were confused. My experience was that learning to drive in Boston was more like a nightmare!

"Really?" I thought. "Studying the Bible can't be *that* dangerous!"

Lisa explained. "When I first started working," she said, "I had an apartment in East Boston and traveled all over the city for work and fun, using the T." (The "T" is how Bostonians affectionately refer to the subway system.)

"Later, when I moved to the suburbs and bought a car, I began driving the roads that overlaid that very subway system, and for a while it seemed I had to entirely relearn the city. Nothing was familiar to me, and it took a long time to connect what I knew so well *underground* to the streets and buildings and distances between places *aboveground*.

"It's been the same process for me in studying the Bible. Early on, I learned a few key foundational truths to undergird my faith. I was so excited to learn the truths in Jeremiah 29:11, then go underground and come up to Psalm 23, and then learn about Revelation 3:20; John 3:16; and Galatians 5:22. But I would zip from one verse to another verse without really understanding the context of where they actually fit in the whole of the Bible. Now, as I am learning the lay of the land, I'm finding those treasured truths amid the context of a much bigger picture."

Lisa wasn't just picking up bits here and there. Our deliberate and intentional study of the Bible was helping her see how it all fit together. This is the key shift that happens when someone is growing. A person no longer relies on random verses that offer encouragement on different topics; they begin to see the whole story of God.

Whether driving in Boston or navigating the spiritual landscape of the kingdom of God, once this level of understanding has been reached, we have a foundation — something that can support the rest of our journey. There is always more that can be learned, but a bigger picture is beginning to form.

READING TO LEARN

There are some parallels between the "learning" of this first stage of spiritual growth and early child development. Early elementary educators typically observe a shift in young children as they grow and mature. In the first year or two of school, the focus of a "reading" curriculum will involve learning the meaning of words, basic grammar, and sentence structure. Children are learning *how* to read. They are comprehending the mechanics of language at a basic level.

And then it changes. Suddenly, the light of comprehension is turned on. Symbols on pages connect to meaningful ideas, to a story, to reality. The child has now learned to read *and* comprehend. But this achievement is hardly the destination; it's simply a significant threshold. It may seem obvious, but after this point, the purpose of reading is to learn. We learn to read; then we read to learn. And once we can read, we can learn anything. The door is opened wide. The same principle applies to the basic truths of the spiritual life. Once we grasp the basics, those basics become foundational to everything else we do.

GOALS OF THE LEARNING TOGETHER STAGE

The Learning Together stage is the initial stage when new believers develop a firm foundation on which they can keep growing for the rest of their lives. In this stage, believers learn some important "rules of the road." They begin to grasp what becoming a disciple of Jesus might actually hold for them — especially when all they've ever known is the kingdom of earth, not the countercultural, upside-down kingdom of heaven. There's a lot to learn, and to unlearn!

Among churches that have taken the REVEAL survey, the greatest percentage of respondents typically fall into this early stage of spiritual development. Unfortunately, there is no correlation between how long someone has been a follower of Christ and whether or not they remain in the Learning Together stage. Many who have been Christians for years, even decades, stay in this stage. Their responses to REVEAL indicate that though they may be attending church, they are not actively growing.

In this first stage of growth, a person should discover the answers to several key questions:

- Who is God?
- What is God like?
- What has God revealed about himself?
- What are God's intentions in this world?
- Who is Jesus?
- Why is the Bible important?
- What is the Bible all about?
- What does the Bible have to say about my life?

These questions get answered at deeper and deeper levels as we grow, and through a variety of inputs. So in this Learning Together stage, we can identify three goals for learning: (1) Scripture, (2) core beliefs, and (3) ways of relating to God and others.

Learn Scripture

First, we anchor our learning in the Bible. The psalmist writes these words in Psalm 119:

> Blessed are those whose ways are blameless,
>   who walk according to the law of the LORD.
> Blessed are those who keep his statutes
>   and seek him with all their heart—
> they do no wrong
>   but follow his ways.

You have laid down precepts
    that are to be fully obeyed.
Oh, that my ways were steadfast
    in obeying your decrees!

                   — Psalm 119:1–5

Later in this psalm, verse 105 reads, "Your word is a lamp for my feet, a light on my path." If there's anything those who are learning to internalize the basics need, it's a well-lit, well-directed path for their life in Christ.

The State of the Bible 2012 study published by the American Bible Society tells us that 85 percent of American households have a Bible. But 36 percent of Americans read the Bible *less than once a year or never*, while 33 percent read the Bible once a week or more.[1] While this statistic may reflect our general culture, even many believers do not have a strong grasp of the Bible. So one of the primary goals of the Learning Together stage is to build a frame of understanding about the Scriptures and then to learn key truths from within Scripture.

How Strong Is Your Biblical Literacy?

For leaders in the church, hopefully this is a simple test. You might try asking these questions to a few of your acquaintances in your church to find out how much of this is general knowledge outside of leadership circles.*

1. Who wrote the first four books of the New Testament?
2. Who wrote the first five books of the Old Testament?
3. Which two Old Testament books are named for women?
4. What is the Great Commission?
5. What is the book of Acts about?

* For more biblical literacy questions, see appendix 3 or visit www.probe.org/site/c.fdKEIMNsEoG/b.4221247/k.261/Bible_Literacy_Quiz.htm (accessed March 1, 2013).

6. Which angel appeared to Mary?
7. Who was known as the wisest man in the world?
8. Which city fell after the Israelites marched around it daily for seven days?
9. What did God give the Israelites to eat in the wilderness?
10. What was Jesus' first miracle?

How did you do? How did they do? If you're stumped on any questions, go to appendix 3 to see the answers on page 176. If you'd like to try answering a few more questions, see pages 175–176.

Learn Core Beliefs

Someone like my friend Frank won't simply show up at a few Sigma Chi Bible studies and suddenly understand with perfect clarity everything about the deity of Christ. A person new to faith is unlikely to have any clear beliefs about the authority of the Bible. So, along with developing a growing familiarity with Scripture, a growing believer learns core beliefs that are vitally important for the rest of their spiritual journey. According to the REVEAL research, these five core beliefs are critical in the early stages of growth:

1. Salvation by grace
2. Existence of the Trinity
3. Authority of Scripture
4. Kindness of God
5. Everlasting love of God

Learn to Relate to God and Others

Finally, in addition to forging a relationship with God, people in the Learning Together stage need to form healthy, life-giving, nurturing bonds with other Christians — relationships that are accepting, God-focused, and fun. These relationships are increasingly rare both in our culture at large and in the church, but they hold great potential for exponential growth.

This kind of relationship made all the difference for Brian.

Brian moved to Chicago after graduating from college and had been living in the city about nine months. In his own words, he was on the right career path but the wrong life path.

"A friend kept asking me to go to church, but I was not interested," Brian explained. "Then I reached a low point and agreed to go. I don't remember the message or much about the service that day, but I remember meeting some cool people."

That week, after attending the church service, Brian couldn't sleep. He felt emotionally unsettled, like something was stirring in his heart. He returned to the church the following week. After the service, people were invited to gather into their small groups, but Brian didn't have a small group. Neither did seminary student Tyler Grissom, who happened to be visiting the church that day as well. Brian and Tyler met and sat together in the lobby. That's when they discovered a shared interest in country music and cowboy boots.

"We knew in that moment that we'd be friends," Tyler said.

Tyler shared part of his faith journey with Brian and then asked Brian if he'd talk about his, assuming that Brian was also a Christ follower. So it came as quite a surprise when Brian's first words to Tyler were, "I'm lost." Tyler's authenticity and vulnerability in sharing his own story enabled Brian to be completely honest as well. "I don't have a story," Brian admitted. "I know a little about God, but I'm pretty confused. If someone could help me understand what a relationship with God is all about, I'm ready to listen."

That was not what Tyler had expected! Trusting that this was a divine appointment, he used Romans 6:23 to share the gospel with Brian and explained the meaning of words like *wages*, *sin*, *death*, *life*, and *gift*. Tyler asked Brian several questions to make sure Brian really understood the gospel.

"I was incredibly hungry and seeking," Brian said recently, as he and Tyler retold their story. "I knew there was more."

After a long discussion in the church lobby, Tyler sensed Brian was ready to trust Christ. "Do you want to do this right now?" he asked.

"I just about screamed a prayer!" Brian recalls. Brian's life immediately began to change. The old patterns were replaced by new habits of pursuing God—and the people who knew him noticed.

Most of the time, this is how the story ends. Brian has been saved, and we assume that in some mysterious way he will grow into a mature Christ follower. Tyler's role has been played. But Tyler knew this wasn't the end of the story; it was just the beginning of his journey. And it's a journey best carried out together, with others. So Tyler arranged to visit with Brian the following week—simply to reconnect.

Tyler sat and listened to me . . . again," Brian said. "I couldn't believe someone cared for me. The fact that he came back the next week was so huge to me. He helped me stay on track."

"I was so drawn to Brian's story," Tyler says, "and wanted to walk with him. I had seen people come to faith before but had never journeyed with someone beyond that point. I watched Brian be transformed and it's been cool to be a part of that. First Peter 3:15 tells us to always be prepared to share our faith. If I had not been prepared or had backed off, I think our stories would have taken a different turn." Tyler continued sharing his faith with Brian, building and developing their newly formed relationship in Christ.

Five years have passed. The two men have become good friends. They've stood up in each other's weddings and shared the highs and lows of life together. When Tyler's dad was suddenly killed in an accident, Brian was one of the first people Tyler's wife called, and he immediately headed over to comfort his friend.

"Our story is a picture of what it means to be the church and it's a story that is still being written," Tyler said. "I know we'll stay connected for the long haul. People often ask us if we're brothers. I hope someday we're old men in rocking chairs, reminiscing about all our stories along the way." And still wearing their cowboy boots and listening to their favorite country music, of course.

The changes in Brian's life were more than changes to his lifestyle. Brian grew in his faith journey by studying the deep truths about God. He was taught different ways of relating to God (Bible study, prayer, etc.) that will equip him for the rest of his life with God. His grasp of Scripture as an authority for his life will provide him with guidance and direction for the road ahead. And he'll be used by God to help others who, just like he once was, are confused and searching for answers to the meaning of life.

That's the goal of the Learning Together stage. New believers take steps of growth, learning what it means to follow Christ and learning *from other believers* how to think and act like a disciple of Jesus.

WHAT'S STIRRING?

1. What is there about this stage that you can point to as being most important in your own life?

2. Who if anyone helped you in this stage of your own growth? Think about this person and, if possible, send a note or make a phone call, thanking him or her for the investment made in your life.

3. As you think of your current relationships, who may be in this first stage of the journey? Have you been available to them as they grow? How can you support and encourage their growth?

CHAPTER 2
BUILD THE FOUNDATION

For the past three years, our home has been packed with high school students every Thursday night. The adults who lead this student gathering always thank us for opening our home, but the fact is, my husband and I are usually upstairs thanking God! We simply marvel at these adults who care so much about our kids and their friends, even until very late in the evening. But these leaders don't seem to mind at all. They love what they do, and they love those kids.

In the last chapter, we began talking about the first stage of spiritual growth — the Learning Together stage. It's a stage that has many challenges, but it can also be great fun. It's rewarding to see transformation happening right before your eyes. It's like having a front-row seat to the miraculous power of God, watching people change and mature in their faith. Language gets cleaned up; poor lifestyle patterns are broken, while new, healthy disciplines and habits are established. Priorities shift and values are developed. God's world is a big new adventure, and there's much to learn and see and touch and taste.

I remember vividly seeing the lightbulb come on in Pam's eyes. She was a new believer and was reading through Philippians with me when she suddenly realized how much God actually cared about her—personally. The truth of God's Word began to seep into her heart, and it led to changes that radically altered her life.

Years ago, I led a small group for several women who, like Pam, were in this early stage of growth. The clever name for our group was "The Tuesday Night Women's Group." At the end of our study, we bequeathed the office room where we met to a men's small group that needed the space, and as we wrote a blessing to leave for the guys, we thought it would be cool to sign the names of all the women who had, over the seven years we had met, been a part of our group. There were never more than eight women in the group at any given time, so we were stunned to realize thirty-two names were listed at the bottom of the page. Thirty-two lives had shared their Learning Together season and grown into the next stage of their journey with God.

Now, years later, most of these women are still following Christ—often leading others—and I'm grateful to know I was a part of their story in an important season of growth in which they built a solid faith foundation.

SIGNS OF LIFE

We can expect to observe four things in individuals as they move through this stage of growth:

1. *God-awareness.* Growing believers in the first stage of spiritual formation show an increasing ability to connect what's going on in their daily life with what they're experiencing and learning about in their spiritual life. This is huge!
2. *Personal encouragement.* Growing believers experience newfound encouragement as they meet with God directly in Scripture.
3. *Openness to God's wisdom.* An increased openness to receiving guidance from God through the Bible and others marks this stage.

4. *New attitudes and behaviors.* God's presence and activity become noticeable as the fruit of the Spirit is increasingly expressed in their lives and relationships.

It's a thrill to see these signs of life in people you're leading. In this chapter, I'll offer practical ideas that can help you help others grow through this important stage of spiritual development. And, as foundational as this stage is, it's not enough for people to remain in this stage. With this in mind, we'll explore some of the dangers of the things that can happen—in individual lives and in faith communities—when people get stuck in this stage of growth.

How can we offer the very best relational support possible to someone in the Learning Together stage? First we'll look at what level of direction a beginner needs and where discernment is needed. Then we'll explore the kinds of relationships that are most helpful for people in this stage, as well as reviewing a variety of relational formats that can welcome and nurture the spiritual growth of those in this stage.

BALANCING DIRECTION AND DISCERNMENT

In the Learning Together stage, as in all three stages, people need relationships that provide them with both direction and discernment. Since the goals involve the acquisition of many important truths, the proportion of direction to discernment is heavily weighted toward direction.

Spiritual Transformation in Relationships

| STAGE 1: | Stage 2: | Stage 3: |
| Learning Together | Journeying Together | Following Together |

Direction

As you can see in the diagram, relationships in this stage entail giving a lot of specific direction, as much as 90 percent. While much helpful content has already been written about effectively leading a small group, I offer three key ideas to keep in mind:

1. Set the right environment for your meetings and time spent together.
2. Establish an effective structure for your relationship.
3. Offer practical helps in developing a day-to-day life with God.

The Right Environment

The right environment is one that is both relationally *and* spiritually welcoming. People in early stages of their faith journey are often stepping into new environments, so it is especially important that you work to create a welcoming atmosphere. From the start, they will have a strong need to feel accepted and know that they belong.

I come from a large Irish family, and I've always loved this Irish welcome:

Come in the evening, come in the morning,
Come when expected, come without warning.
Thousands of welcomes you'll find here before you.
And the oftener you come, the more we'll adore you!

I especially like the last line and what it communicates: *The more we get to know you, the more we'll love you.* That's exactly the kind of relational environment that you as a leader want those you serve to experience!

In addition to being relationally welcoming, we should seek to maintain an atmosphere of spiritual welcome. This means that no matter where people find themselves in their relationship with God, we embrace them with open arms, a welcoming smile, and an extended hand, as well as showing them an inclusive attitude that avoids condemnation. A spiritual welcome conveys that people at all stages of the spiritual journey (and particularly the early stage) have a place among us.

I remember hearing of an awkward moment in one small group when a high-powered executive in the entertainment industry showed up. It was his first small group experience. His wife had been pleading with him for years, and it took every bit of courage for him to show up at a neighbor's house on a weeknight. Not knowing his background, another couple in the group began spouting off about "the intolerable trash" that's on television during the "getting to know you" question time. After finishing their tirade, someone in the group turned to the executive and asked him, "So what do you do for a living?" It was too late. The damage had already been done. He never returned to the group.

In contrast to this example, the high school group that meets in our basement showed maturity beyond their years when they reversed a decision about what to study one summer. In an effort to maintain a spiritually welcoming environment for newcomers, they shifted their plans to study the book of Revelation and chose the gospel of Matthew instead. Though many of them were interested in Revelation, they concluded that one of the Gospels would be a better introduction to the Bible and the Christian faith.

None of this is complicated or radical. But it reminds us that when our hearts are tuned to care for the growth of people, we will think about the spiritual environment we create for their growth and learning. We need to respect where people are at and seek to recognize the spiritual needs of those who are still forming their core beliefs.

An Effective Structure

Like anyone embarking on a new journey or learning a new environment, those in the Learning Together stage need direction and boundaries. They need to know their group is safe, gathers regularly and on time, and meets them where they are. Some people prefer to meet in a group setting, while others choose one-on-one relationships. It's important to offer both opportunities — not just a single small group structure.

It's also important to have a good directive curriculum or study guide that will address those foundational goals. This helps provide a solid structure in both groups and one-on-one meetings.[1] While free-flowing conversation about life can be fun and interesting, it isn't as helpful for those who haven't yet formed the structures of truth that will undergird their long-term development. Since it's not part of our normal conversation to talk about the Trinity or the authority of Scripture or several of the other important and basic truths we need to learn, it helps to have a plan — something to guide those conversations.

Practical Helps for Day-to-Day Life with God

At my church, I recently facilitated what had been promoted as an advanced-level class on prayer. I was excited to teach people I assumed would be mature believers. I planned to talk about various kinds of prayer that can be transforming and helpful in some of the later stages of spiritual development. I prepared my lessons, eager to take the class to the deep end of the prayer pool.

The first week we met, I started our time together by asking what questions they had about prayer. I was stunned when the first person said, "I don't know how to pray. I know Christians are supposed to pray, but I've never learned." Several others echoed his comments, and I knew I would have to quickly and completely adjust my teaching plan.

While many believers are hungry to learn the basics, they do not always know where to turn for help. I'm also discovering that many end up turning to non-Christian spiritual sources when they can't find help in learning the basics of biblical thought and the discipline of prayer.

My point is simple: people in this foundation-laying stage need practical teaching that shows them how to walk with God day by day. It's vital to intentionally teach the basic spiritual practices, such as reflection on Scripture, Bible study, simple prayer, and making connections with a spiritual friend. It's our responsibility to help people see how relationships with God and with others make possible the process of ongoing spiritual growth.

Five Questions Leaders Can Ask

1. What have you been learning about God lately?
2. What is a passage of Scripture that has opened your eyes to a new truth about God?
3. How are you experiencing prayer these days? Is it easy or hard to pray?
4. What has changed most in your understanding of the Christian life since you first became a Christian?
5. What has felt confusing lately in your relationship with God?

Discernment

While those who are serving individuals in the Learning Together stage will primarily offer a directive style of relationship, it is still vitally important for them to offer the gifts of discernment, particularly as those individuals begin to mature. A concerned leader is in a unique position to see what few others can see. And they can especially offer two important observations to those in this stage: (1) notice, name, and encourage spiritual progress; and (2) notice when people are ready to move on to the next stage of growth.

1. Notice, name, and encourage spiritual progress. Often, it's hard to notice changes in ourselves. We may need other people to recognize that we've changed and to call it out. Someone who truly helps their growth will notice and draw attention to these shifts and changes in attitudes, behavior, or reliance on God. Like a mirror, we reflect back to them the spiritual progress we observe in them. This not only helps them be grateful for the work that God is doing, but it also encourages their ongoing growth and trust in God. All of us can begin to lose hope at times that we're experiencing any growth at all—and the loving perspective of a leader can remind us of God's activity and show us how far we've come.

2. Notice when people are ready to move on to the next stage. Another important area of discernment involves watching for indicators that people are ready to take some important next steps. You may hear them make statements like these:

- *I want more of God.* When a person says, "There just has to be more," you can be sure the Holy Spirit is doing a new thing. As a leader, you want to find out what that's about. The hunger for more is always something to pay attention to.
- *I want to be different.* Sometimes brokenness catapults people into the next stage of growth. Because people often get stuck in the Learning Together stage, pain, addiction, or wounds can serve as catalysts that lead them into the next steps of the journey.
- *I've hit a wall.* When people hit a wall, they're wrestling with difficult questions and issues. You'll hear them say things like, "I know a lot about the Bible, but I'm not growing." "I've read the Bible, but I'm not moving forward." "I don't want to go through the motions anymore." "I'm just not satisfied with pat answers." "I feel stuck and stalled in my spiritual growth."
- *I'm bored with the group.* People may complain that they're tired of the material. They may even dread going to group meetings.

Discerning this readiness to move on may be the most essential element you add to your existing process of spiritual formation. Develop a process that will help you identify those who have stalled in their growth, and find out what is blocking them from taking the next step forward.

Let's now look at how to find the right relational format for those you lead.

FINDING THE RIGHT RELATIONAL FORMAT

At various times in this chapter, as I've written about the right relationships for people going through the Learning Together stage, I've used the term *leader.* That's not a mistake. People in this stage need a specific type of relationship to facilitate growth—a relationship with someone we might call a leader or mentor, someone to walk alongside them who will wisely direct them toward appropriate information and experiences they need in order to mature. The leader should be further into their own journey and be capable of leading through a process.

Here are a few examples of relational formats that can be helpful for people in this early stage of Learning Together. I'm also offering basic definitions, though I hope these are clear to everyone.

Small Group. A small group is a gathering of several people who desire to build community and grow spiritually. Churches also call this a life group, community group, or home group. Small groups are useful ways of making a big church feel small. They also provide opportunities for outreach or service. Most often, a strong curriculum is provided or chosen by the group.

Bible Study. A Bible study focuses on the study of Scripture. This can happen in a large group or a small one—but typically a Bible study involves some discussion and interaction as part of the learning process. Bible studies are great for not only growing in biblical literacy but also forming relationships with other group members.

Alpha Group. Alpha guides participants through a specific process for learning core beliefs of the Christian faith. Alpha addresses questions like, "Who is Jesus?" "Who is the Holy Spirit?" "Why and how should I read the Bible?" "How do I pray?" Churches around the world use the engaging curriculum that points people to God's truth. In addition to providing great content, the experience is designed to give participants an experience of community.

One-on-One Discipleship. One-on-one discipleship is a way for one believer to encourage spiritual growth in another by spending time with them and intentionally talking about their life, questions, and next steps in faith. In order to be helpful to the Learning Together stage, this relationship should be supported by a process (curriculum or study guide) designed to cover foundational elements.

You may be familiar with most of these examples. Of the three stages, the Learning Together stage is the one most churches focus on as they address the journey of spiritual growth. Let me emphasize that these four examples are not meant to be exhaustive. Your church may have other kinds of groups or structures in place.

The goal of all these structures and programs is to "get people moving" in their spiritual journey. Greg Hawkins and Cally Parkinson summarize the best practices of the churches that effectively disciple new believers: "Best practice churches promote and provide a high-impact, nonnegotiable pathway of focused first steps—a pathway designed specifically to jump-start a spiritual experience that gets people moving toward a Christ-centered life."[2]

In addition to reviewing a variety of different formats, churches also need to be sure that entry points into these kinds of groups are readily available and obvious to those who are ready for this next step. The most difficult aspect can sometimes be accurately and clearly communicating to those who attend your church how to take the first step in their spiritual journey.

FINDING THE RIGHT LEADERS

What matters most in all of this is having well-equipped leaders who can meet growing believers exactly where and as they are and who will possess the leadership strength to *directively* lead them through this stage.

Strong relational support for this stage begins with leaders who demonstrate genuine care and interest in others' journey with God. There is a wide world in front of Christ followers in this stage. Especially if they are new to the faith, they're eager to grow, but they need guides who are attuned to their needs. The table below identifies key leadership qualities and spiritual gifts for effective small group leaders and mentors who can walk with new believers on this journey.

Leadership Qualities	Spiritual Gifts[3]
• Adequate knowledge of material and ability to explain truths well • Willingness to share one's own story with authenticity • Easily approachable	• Teaching • Shepherding • Encouragement • Leadership

Both small group leaders and participants benefit from understanding that different stages of spiritual growth require different kinds of spiritual relationships, experiences, and disciplines. And leaders will be encouraged and relieved to know it's actually a *good* thing when people outgrow their need for one kind of relational environment and move on to another kind of group or mentoring relationship. Communicate to your small group leaders that they have not failed if people end their participation in a group, particularly if that person moves on to develop other types of relationships in the church. Not only is this not a reflection of failure on the part of the small group leader; it is likely a significant indicator of success!

As we will see in upcoming chapters, having a clear vision of how transformation happens in the context of relationships sets up a new expectation—that while ongoing spiritual growth will continue to happen in community, the kind of community each person needs will change as a reflection of God's natural path for spiritual development in the body of Christ (see Ephesians 4:1–16).

WHAT IF PEOPLE DON'T MOVE ON?

When individuals or whole churches get stuck in the Learning Together stage, everyone suffers. When they're stuck, people can end up doing these three things: (1) become arrogant about what they've learned (to the point of harming the cause of Christ), (2) give up on any hope of growth and change, or (3) remain immature.

1. They become arrogant and harm the cause of Christ. The defining feature of the Learning Together stage is the acquisition of knowledge. Consequently, those who are stuck in this stage tend to elevate, above all else, knowledge as the virtue of maturity. They believe that if you know a lot, you're mature. From there, smug self-righteousness breeds all manner of negative energy. In such a community, what matters most is what you know, not what kind of person you are or the kind of impact you're having on the world around you.

In their book *unchristian*, authors David Kinnaman and Gabe Lyons offer a sobering word to the body of Christ.[4] The authors suggest that the lack of transformation in the church is actually doing damage to the name of Christ. How? If we substitute head knowledge for authentic spiritual growth, we abandon the path of transformation and instead become hypocritical, judgmental, or self-righteous. And while knowing truth is important (after all, it's a key goal of this stage), an overemphasis on knowledge can inadvertently prevent us the deeper journey of transformation.

2. They give up on the hope of growth and change. After some time, if we experience ourselves as growing, we end up feeling discouraged and frustrated, stalled in our relationship with God. And some who remain stagnant for a long time eventually *give up.* Sometimes they stay in the church, but often they leave.

Those who stay in the church and continue going through the motions are no longer on an adventure with God. They have abandoned the pursuit of any new growth. Spiritually speaking, they're just punching the clock. It's not that they're necessarily doing harm to the cause, but neither are they living the dream God has for them. The cause of Christ suffers from their absence. Their heads may be full of good theology, but their hearts are empty of hope.

3. They remain immature. Though this overlaps with the first two consequences stated, I want to say it bluntly: when someone gets stuck, they do not become what, or who, they might have become. All of us have been given a race that's marked out for us, but some miss the race or run the wrong one. Each of us has a choice. We can either engage or not. Sadly, though, everyone loses out when believers do not "own" their journey.

GETTING STUCK, IN REAL LIFE

Over the years, I've heard various versions of the same story. An individual has been serving, even in vocational ministry, for several years and has been in a relationship with God since an early age. Yet some form of sin, some self-destructive pattern, led to deeply ingrained habits of hiding and shame. Despite learning the great truths about God in early stages of development, there is no one to guide further progress into the journey of brokenness and transformation. Even as knowledge about God increases, these folks grow ever more despondent over behaviors they could not change. Habits of hiding and shame become a way of life.

From that place of shame, we are tempted by the periodic effort to "power up" and overcome sinful habits through rigorous behavior modification. Short-lived "success" comes after focusing on self-effort and refining methods of sin management. But the cost — one's heart and one's hope in the power of God — takes its toll.

One such friend shared, "About ten years ago, I just stopped trying. I stopped reading my Bible. I stopped bothering." Why? Because "trying" didn't work anymore. It only brought exhaustion, frustration, and more shame.

I'm convinced he and others like him will never leave the faith. He still believes, very deeply, that Jesus is the way to God, that there is a world of great importance around us, and that God is at work. But he has opted out of transformation. Even though he works for a church, no one has seemed to notice that he has settled into a long stall, that he has stopped maturing and growing. Although he's been a Christian for many years, he got stuck in the earliest stage of spiritual growth and has remained there ever since. I can't help but wonder how his life might have been different had his brokenness been met with a life-giving path for transformation rather than a process of soul-stifling sin management.

Recently, there have been some encouraging signs, as he has taken the first steps on a new path, one I hope will help him transition from simply *knowing facts about* God to *knowing* God. As we will soon see, he will be moving from Learning Together to Journeying Together. This second stage will be a very personal journey and a messier process. Sometimes the path to grow in faith looks and feels *worse* before it gets *better*.

As followers of Christ, we know we will continue learning for the rest of our lives. But we grow and mature from simply learning about God when we move from the despair of sin management to the hope of authentic transformation. This occurs when we learn to face our own inner brokenness and failure, and help others in this process as well.

When we're not put off by the struggles that people carry, we create new space for God to do what only God can do.

TRANSITIONING TO THE NEXT STAGE

To best help those in the Learning Together stage, there's one final thing you can uniquely do for them: provide a bridge to the next stage. What types of relationships will these growing believers need in order to continue growing? For many who reach this transition point, they aren't sure where to turn after having traveled the well-worn path of Bible study groups.

But wise leaders know a new stage of spiritual growth is beckoning—the Journeying Together stage. Be intentional about helping your people get there. Much is at stake if you don't. Remember, this was just the beginning.

WHAT'S STIRRING?

1. Have you ever led a group, or an individual, through the Learning Together stage? Who was it, and how did your lives become connected? What did you enjoy about serving them in this stage? What was difficult about it? Where is that person now?

2. How well does your current ministry context support this stage with appropriate relational and spiritual environments?

3. Can you relate to the idea of getting stuck in this stage? Who or what, if anything, helped you get unstuck and keep moving?

PART 2

JOURNEYING TOGETHER

CHAPTER 3
OWN THE JOURNEY

Usually, when we think of owning something, we think of physical objects such as a car, a pair of jeans, or a house. If we are mature, we assume responsibility for it. It's ours to enjoy, and it's ours to take care of. If we don't assume ownership, these objects fall into disrepair, and we'll miss out on what we otherwise might have enjoyed.

Can you imagine finding out you are the rightful owner of a home, only to discover that it had been ignored and left exposed to the elements for years? How might it have served your family? What stability and protection might you have enjoyed by using it? What kinds of taxes and penalties might you owe? How might that house have been improved over time instead of allowed to crumble?

As responsible adults, we also "own" our choices, our attitudes, our behaviors. And depending on how well we steward our ownership of those things, they, too, can either contribute to our lives or fall into disrepair. To help us take ownership over interior realities, for example, twelve-step recovery programs use a great expression for the fourth step: taking a *moral inventory*. Like a warehouse owner, we need to know what's actually inside, understand what we have done, and take responsibility for the consequences of our choices. During this step, it's necessary to resist the temptation to focus on what other people have done—however tempting—and remain focused on our own deeds.

But this idea of "owning up" doesn't just involve bringing hidden or harmful patterns into the light. Jesus' parable in Matthew 25 also challenges us to "own" the things we have been given by God, whether they are material or immaterial. The servants are judged according to what they did with what they were given. God expects us to assume responsibility.

Those who have progressed through the Learning Stage eventually transition into a stage marked by this quality: *taking ownership*. To this point, a Christ follower is focused on receiving and learning—being a student of the faith. And this, obviously, continues to be a key quality contributing to ongoing growth and maturity. But the next significant stage of growth and development in the spiritual formation process happens as disciples of Jesus take ownership of two very important immaterial things: (1) their day-by-day life with God, and (2) their interior world, including their journey.

Those who make this transition can become deep, centered individuals who are marked by increased humility, spiritual power, and natural expressions of the character qualities of Jesus. Those who do not make this transition, sadly, remain locked into acquiring head knowledge about God but do not develop the capacity to be shaped by God. There are no shortcuts, but interior transformation is absolutely the goal.

GOD'S WILL FOR OUR LIVES

When we ask, "What is God's will for my life?" we are usually asking because we want an answer to a specific choice we have to make—things like "Whom should I date? Or marry?" "Where should I go to school?" "What job should I take?" or "What's my life's work/ministry supposed to be?" These are all terrific questions to think about, and those who are wise will seek God's direction. But there is one area of our lives in which God's intention for us is quite clear. It's sometimes so obvious we miss it. It is always God's will for us to become mature—becoming more like Christ in our thoughts, actions, and character. The old-fashioned but deeply meaningful word for this process is *sanctification*. "It is God's will that you should be sanctified" (1 Thessalonians 4:3). God's intended desire is that we become newly shaped people—from the inside out—growing more and more into the likeness of Jesus. Bottom line: God cares not only about what we are *doing*; equally important, he cares about who we are *becoming*. The ongoing miracle of real transformation is that we begin, naturally, to do what Jesus would do if he were living our lives in our place.

So while God's will for us may include particular gifts, talents, and assignments that are unique to our lives, God also gives every believer the common goal of spiritual maturity. As we'll see later, our growth in *doing* and our growth in *becoming* are actually deeply connected. This is the realm of spiritual formation—the interior development of character, of soul. As Bill Hybels once said at an evangelism conference, this interior development causes people to naturally "love what Jesus loves, disdain what Jesus disdains, have compassion on what Jesus has compassion on, forgive what Jesus would forgive."

God, in his wisdom, equips us for the road ahead by deepening our capacities for love and preparing us for the assignments he has for us. Unfortunately, many on this road have never made this journey into the realm of their interior life with God. In my work with leaders, I've been saddened to discover some who truly love God and have given years of their lives in sacrificial service but have never probed the deeper places of the soul. As a result, they are poorly equipped for the challenges they encounter. It is necessary to go to these places if we want to grow and mature in our faith.

GOALS OF THE JOURNEYING TOGETHER STAGE

Thankfully, we don't have to journey alone, though many do. When the church is working right, God uses our relationships with other people to help us along this new stage of interior soul work. These relationships become like desert guides for our journey—wise fellow journeyers who have also traversed some of the unseen and often barren places in life and who can now help us travel a path we might not have noticed or chosen on our own.

Where do people develop these relationships? Some people encounter them in unlikely or unexpected situations. A desert guide might be a sponsor in a twelve-step community, or it can be an ordinary friendship that, in the face of tragedy, suddenly deepens and grows. Significant guidance can also be found through reading books and learning from the inner journeys of others, even those who lived centuries before our time (see appendix 4). While these stories and experiences can greatly aid the inner journey, ideal spiritual growth is supported by an "in-person" guide, a soul caretaker who can help you personally face your brokenness and come face-to-face with the God you have been learning about.

This middle stage of spiritual growth deals in the unseen realm and often begins with some disappointment and disillusionment. Many who find themselves here wish they could skip it entirely. Why? Because life in this middle place can be confusing and hard, though essential to maturity. Novelist Sue Monk Kidd accurately describes our tendency to devalue what she calls the "middle places": "We seem to have focused so much on exuberant beginnings and victorious endings that we've forgotten about the slow, sometimes tortuous, unraveling of God's grace that takes place in the 'middle places.'"[1] As you'll see, this stage absolutely depends on the unraveling of God's grace.

Owning the journey involves a lot of self-discovery. Who knew these places even existed within us? Whether we were reluctant to explore the interior world or simply unaware, the new avenues of self-discovery highlight the two goals of the Journeying Together stage: (1) discovering the depth of our soul's ongoing need for God as we develop new ways of staying open to God and (2) discovering the unseen dynamics of our interior world as we embark on paths of healing and restoration.

Discovering Our Need for God

I've not done much underwater diving, but I know enough to understand this: if you want to swim in the deep places of the ocean, you will need the right equipment and you need to use it. Your moment-by-moment connection to an oxygen tank will be the only thing that makes the underwater journey possible. You will naturally and gladly *depend* on that equipment as your source of life. No one has to convince a diver one hundred feet under water to use their tank. Below the surface, that tank is their life. They are fully aware of their dependency.

As we grow spiritually, a similar possibility opens up to us. We discover a capacity to depend on God, moment by moment. Like the diver's practice of breathing through a mouthpiece and tube, there are practices of connection with God that make the deep spiritual journey possible. We develop rhythms of attachment, dependency, and receptivity to God that acknowledge our true need for God. We make peace with this simple but profound declaration that Moses gave to the Israelites long ago: "For the LORD is your life" (Deuteronomy 30:20). And as we grow in our capacity to connect with God, the Holy Spirit increasingly leads and empowers us moment by moment, day by day. We depend on God's whispers, wisdom, and ways more and more. Increasingly, we are conscious and aware that "in him we live and move and have our being" (Acts 17:28).

To be clear, our need for God is not a new concept. In the Learning Together stage, we became well acquainted with our fundamental need for God. We have grasped the depth of our sinfulness and our need for God's righteousness. In the Journeying Together stage, though, we hunger for God's person and presence—right now, right here. We discover God as our source of life, like a vine is the source of life for its branches (John 15:5). There is no life for a branch outside of a meaningful, ongoing connection to that vine. Owning our need to connect with God becomes our priority. Intellectual growth and head knowledge are no longer sufficient—we have an ache in our soul to *know* God, not simply to *know about* God. Just as we would a close friend.

We relate to God as a person, not as facts or data—as true as they may be. So in the Journeying Together phase, we grow in our capacity to experience God through several core spiritual practices, all of which take time and intentionality to learn. We gladly embrace the responsibility to remain meaningfully connected. We begin to grasp that it's not the responsibility of our pastor, our friend, or even our spouse to grow us and mature us; it's *our* job. Finally, we no longer see this responsibility as a tedious chore of working our way through spiritual disciplines. Nor, any longer, do we expect this deep relationship with God to be something the church does for us through programs or classes, though we may continue to participate in those.

As we become more deeply connected to Christ, moment by moment, day by day, we become increasingly open to the Holy Spirit's work within us. The result of a growing connection to God is nothing short of miraculous! We not only receive life; we receive new life. That deep transformational work will always remain God's job. This is how the process of spiritual formation reshapes us into the character of Jesus. Our part is to remain connected.

For most of us, this means we will learn new spiritual rhythms and practices. Postures of attentiveness, attunement, and surrender to the Spirit do not come naturally. Instead, we tend to favor self-protection, image management, and self-directed living. Even with a "Christian" veneer, having learned quite a bit in our spiritual journey, we often want life on our terms. When we don't get our way, we react badly. These all-too-human tendencies must die if we are to take up our cross, as Jesus commands us to do, and follow him. As the character of Christ is formed in us, we ever so gradually become free of self-directed living.[2]

Many helpful and important spiritual practices can be learned during this stage. Individual practices such as prayer, engaging Scripture, spiritual friendship, solitude, soul-searching (examen), and simplicity can be a great place to start when learning new rhythms of dependence on God.[3] They train us to look to God as our source of life, our power and strength, and our source of unchanging love.

Twelve-step recovery offers another example where individuals who have accepted their level of dependency on God adopt a set of practices to stay connected to their now-recovered life. Those who follow these practices are "working the steps." Anyone is welcome to attend an open twelve-step meeting. "Working the steps," though, often involves a commitment to also join a second group in which the person moves beyond merely listening in on the recovery conversation and begins, with a sponsor, to work the twelve steps himself or herself. Sometimes these groups are also referred to as "AWOL" groups—consisting of those who have made recovery "A Way of Life."

That acronym is a perfect description of this "discovering your need for God" stage of the spiritual growth process as well. For those in the Journeying Together stage, the development of a life with God and the spiritual practices that support it become a way of life—a connection that keeps us open to transformation. Biblical texts repeatedly affirm this vision of the Christian faith as a *way of life* that includes a grasp of basic doctrine but extends beyond our agreement with a set of beliefs:

- For this reason I have sent to you Timothy, my son whom I love, who is faithful in the Lord. He will remind you of my *way of life* in Christ Jesus, which agrees with what I teach everywhere in every church.

  — 1 Corinthians 4:17, emphasis added

- That, however, is not the *way of life* you learned when you heard about Christ and were taught in him in accordance with the truth that is in Jesus.

  — Ephesians 4:20–21, emphasis added

- You, however, know all about my teaching, my *way of life*, my purpose, faith, patience, love, endurance ...

  — 2 Timothy 3:10, emphasis added

- Remember your leaders, who spoke the word of God to you. Consider the outcome of their *way of life* and imitate their faith.

  — Hebrews 13:7, emphasis added

The writers of Scripture repeatedly affirm that following Jesus results in an entirely new way of life, not merely the acceptance of a body of ideas that we hear and understand. This is why we must develop habits and practices that shape not only our understanding but also our interior world. Taking ownership for our journey through development of a deep, ongoing connection with God is the first of two goals for the Journeying Together stage.

Discovering Our Interior World

The second key aspect of owning the journey is discovering the hidden forces at work in our interior world—our motives, desires, shame, and fear. For example, a pastor or leader entering this stage of growth may need to come to grips with how their choices, behaviors, and pursuit of God and ministry have been driven by things like family of origin issues, or their own weaknesses and failures. Naming these interior realities—owning them—takes time and intentionality.

Those who progress through this stage of growth gradually learn to own their story—the good, the bad, and the ugly. They discover that all the great facts they've accumulated about God haven't eradicated the darkness that lurks inside. Breakthrough comes when they are willing to face those parts they are most inclined to hide. This is soul work, embracing the brokenness that ultimately shapes them into people who can do what God is inviting them to do in this world.

In this stage, our own brokenness becomes more obvious and unsettling. By now, we well *know* Jesus' teaching on forgiveness, but if we're honest, we can't seem to actually forgive the people we most need to forgive. We *know* God loves us deeply, but the actual shape of our interior world reflects self-hatred and shame. We *know* God wants us to build loving relationships, but we're stuck in patterns of relational dysfunction in which our attempts to improve relationships actually seem to make them worse. We *know* the Holy Spirit alone should govern our actions and words, but we're trapped in the clutches of hidden addictions that numb our pain.

We can respond to these frustrating tensions with increased pretense or perhaps a willful resolve to self-improve, and many in the church choose these options. The step of growth is to translate our frustration with ourselves into a stage of growth through greater dependence on God. We bravely face reality and learn to find God's grace where we least expect it. As we own what is true about us—our brokenness and failure—we become open to God's intervention and healing.

Facing brokenness is never easy. We need help to effectively identify and name the root of our shame or trauma. We also need help to believe that unfailing love, true healing, and new life are possible. In *The Inner Voice of Love*, Henri Nouwen explains how we can face our wounds and our failure in a way that brings transformation:

> The great challenge is *living* your wounds through instead of *thinking* them through. It is better to cry than to worry, better to feel your wounds deeply than to understand them, better to let them enter into your silence than to talk about them. The choice you face constantly is whether you are taking your hurts to your head or to your heart. In your head you can analyze them, find their causes and consequences, and coin words to speak and write about them. But no final healing is likely to come from that source. You need to let your wounds go down into your heart. Then you can live them through and discover that they will not destroy you. Your heart is greater than your wounds.
>
> Understanding your wounds can only be healing when that understanding is put at the service of your heart. Going to your heart with your wounds is not easy; it demands letting go of many questions. You want to know "Why was I wounded? When? How? By whom?" You believe that the answers to these questions will bring relief. But at best they only offer you a little distance from your pain. You have to let go of the need to stay in control of your pain and trust in the healing power of your heart. There your hurts can find a safe place to be received, and once they have been received, they lose their power to inflict damage and become fruitful soil for new life.[4]

Is all this interior work really necessary? Most definitely! Transformation becomes possible as we grow in self-awareness. Psychologist and spiritual formation thought leader Dr. David Benner observes, "You can never be other than who you are until you are willing to embrace the reality of who you are. Only then can you truly become who you are most deeply called to be."[5] In addition, the work God does in healing our wounds—helping us face the things about ourselves or our past that we're scared of and never want to talk to anybody about—these are the things we end up offering to others in love.

We become, as Henri Nouwen describes elsewhere, a "wounded healer." God uses our pain, our inner journey of growth toward maturity in Christ, to minister to the pain and the wounds of others.

> "You can never be other than who you are until you are willing to embrace the reality of who you are. Only then can you truly become who you are most deeply called to be."
>
> **David Benner, *The Gift of Being Yourself***

Because this stage addresses such tender areas of brokenness and healing, it's important that those who lead others have been there themselves. Even if we wanted to, we can't really help others travel a path we haven't traveled ourselves. If we try, we are no better than the proverbial blind guide. Blinded by our own brokenness, we try to help others, not out of our weakness and dependence on God, but out of our self-reliance, pride, and ego. That kind of "help" usually doesn't help at all.

Unless we know ourselves well and have recognized our need for God, we will inadvertently advise others to avoid the desert rather than helping them face their inner neediness and turn to God in honesty. If we have been to the desert ourselves, our help makes all the difference in the world. That's why we need to "journey together." We need companionship in the desert, from real desert guides.

A DESERT JOURNEY

"Mindy, if God takes you to the desert, go there and learn what the desert has to teach."

These were the wise, if unwelcome, words of a trusted spiritual friend. In time, I discovered that those words helped more than any others as I teetered on the edge of this inner journey stage. I can still remember where I stood in my bedroom, talking on the phone with my friend but staring blankly at the bland beige carpet next to the bed. If only the rest of life could be so plain and simple. My world was spinning out of control. And the spinning was more than just a metaphor for the difficult challenges of my life—my body was literally on tilt. If the pain of life gets bad enough, the brain can short-circuit. Mine did, and it manifested as a bad case of vertigo. A few months' worth.

Everything in me resisted my friend's counsel. I did not want to go to the desert. I wanted only one thing: *out*. Out of the desert. Out of the suffering. Out of the confusion. Out of the hopelessness. At the surface, her advice sounded more like giving in or giving up—two things I almost never did. In anything. But deeper possibilities whispered to my imagination through her loving presence and her well-aimed words.

- Could God actually lead me to the desert?
- What would it mean for me to go willingly into this desert—to go as one being led?
- Could it be that there are things for me to learn that can only be learned in a desert?
- Could there be a hidden gift for me in this barrenness?

> **"Maybe, sometimes, in the midst of things going terribly wrong, something is going just right. But that's the devil of it; there is no way to know for sure. All we can do is hope for the dawn."**
>
> **Gerald May, *The Dark Night of the Soul***

I shudder to think how I might have strayed in unwise directions had my friend withheld her keen guidance at this critical time in my life. Throughout that season, she helped me learn to surrender, to yield, and to carefully pay attention to what was going on in the interior realm.

I find that many Christ followers, when facing challenges like this alone, easily stray in unwise and unhelpful directions. To make the interior journey, we need spiritual direction from a trusted guide, because our greatest need is usually not additional knowledge. We need a person who can guide a process of discovery into the dark and hidden realm inside.

DARK NIGHT OF THE SOUL

Several years ago, I came across a book that introduced me to two influential sixteenth-century Spanish mystics—Teresa of Ávila and John of the Cross.[6] These two individuals were contemporaries and colaborers, and each wrote a major work that has become a contemplative classic. Teresa wrote *The Interior Castle*, and John's classic work is titled *The Dark Night of the Soul*.

In my reading I learned that both Teresa and John experienced what they referred to as a "dark night"—a time that is more than just a season of difficulty, as is often assumed. The deeper meaning has been lost in our translation of the word *dark*. Teresa and John did not use *dark* to refer to something sinister or bad—a horrible time filled with pain and suffering. Instead, the Spanish word they used was *oscura*—in English, *obscure*.

> Centuries before Freud "discovered" the unconscious, contemplatives such as Brother Lawrence, Teresa, and John had a profound appreciation that there is an active life of the soul that goes on beneath our awareness. It is to this unconscious dimension of the spiritual life that Teresa and John refer when they use the term "dark" ... For them, it simply means "obscure." In the same way that things are difficult to see at night, the deepest relationship between God and person is hidden from our conscious awareness.
>
> In speaking of *la nocha oscura*, the dark night of the soul, John is addressing something mysterious and unknown, but by no means sinister or evil.[7]

Rather than a time of fear or evil, a "dark night of the soul" season invites us to a time of learning to accept the mystery of things we cannot understand. In our acceptance, we let go of the need to fix or solve what is hidden. Far too often, we want to reject those areas of our lives that we cannot understand or control. Sometimes we confuse what is hidden with what is evil:

> John says it is one thing to be in *oscuras* and quite another to be in *tinieblas* [the sinister kind of darkness]. In *oscuras* things are hidden; in *tinieblas* one is blind. In fact, it is the very blindness of

tinieblas, our slavery to attachment and delusion, that the dark night of the soul is working to heal.[8]

In my own life, the wise counsel of my friend led me to consider that God might be doing some new and important work in the "dark" or obscure regions of my soul. I began to realize I would be wise to allow that work to happen rather than resisting it. I could take ownership of the brokenness and experience a new depth of dependence on God. That's the invitation God offers in this second stage of growth, as we own the journey.

> "This deepening of love is the real purpose of the dark night of the soul. The dark night helps us become who we are created to be: lovers of God and one another."
>
> **Gerald May, *The Dark Night of the Soul***

"Let Nothing Disturb You"

English Translation	Original Spanish
Let nothing disturb you,	Nada te turbe,
Let nothing make you afraid;	nada te espante;
All things pass:	todo se pasa,
God is unchanging.	Dios no se muda.
Patience is enough for everything.	La paciencia todo lo alcanza.
You who have God lack nothing;	Quien a Dios tiene nada le falta:
God alone is sufficient.	solo Dios basta.

Teresa of Ávila, "Bookmark"[9]

HOW ABOUT YOU?

If your own spiritual journey has taken you through the Learning Together stage but not yet beyond it, you may be unfamiliar with some of the concepts introduced in this chapter. Perhaps you've never really let anyone else into your spiritual journey because you've been doing "sole care" as long as you can remember.

Regardless of where you are right now, there is a rewarding adventure ahead if you are willing to embrace the inner journey of deeper dependence on God, even if God takes you to the desert in order to discover it. Almost everyone tries to avoid the desert, and many of us try to deny our need to go there. We don't want to face our own weakness, our own pride, our own self-dependence. We may even grow defensive.

No, I'm not resentful. I'm not hate-filled and jealous and prideful.

Well, yes, you are. Welcome to the inner journey.

Keep in mind that as this stage of growth begins, so do the losses. You may experience a loss of confidence—losing the exhilaration and certainty of faith that come during the Learning Together stage. You may experience a deep disappointment with God or others. For others, it may be an addiction that won't let you go, or character flaws that trap you in patterns that are harmful to those you love. It can be anything that forces you to see that life with God isn't as neat and tidy as you once believed it would be.

We don't unlearn the important truths we've gained; we refine them and test them. As we discover the depths of our self-reliance, our confidence suffers, our certainty is shaken, and our bravado is less sure. Why? In short, we run into a wall. It takes many forms, but whatever version we hit, it's still a wall. We can try running away or retreating; we can try to avoid being broken by it and remain as we are—brittle and unchanging. But if we break in the right ways, we begin to experience God in places we never expected and find that God meets us there. Make no mistake, there is hope beyond the wall. But hitting the wall, well, that's just painful.

We cannot know when it will arrive, but the invitation to intentionally own the journey will come at some point in our lives. The kinds of relationships that surround and support a disciple of Jesus will make all the difference in the world as to whether that journey will be welcomed or pursued or ignored and avoided. It's very difficult to navigate this journey alone.

I end this chapter by sharing the experience of a close friend. Tara is in the midst of owning her faith. Like many high-performing, high-capacity leaders with an overabundance of strengths and talents, she feels comfortable taking care of others and helping them find spiritual support. But it's hard for her to share with others her own struggles, her own needs. She is slowly learning to let others in, to be vulnerable, to depend on God to meet her needs through others.

I grew up as the only child in a non-Christian family—until I turned eleven, and the next five years brought three new siblings and, finally, the end of my parents' marriage. I'll never forget my mom's words: "I'm pregnant again—and your dad and I are getting a divorce." I went from being an only child in a solid family to an only child in a single-parent home with three small siblings.

Thankfully, just as this turbulent season began, I was invited at age twelve to a Christian sports camp. Though I had never met a "Christian" before, by the end of the week I had become one. No doubt, my faith sustained me during hard times.

I began to bury my emotions and found attention and satisfaction in performance. Performance was my drug of choice, and it worked for me. The harder life got, the harder I ran. In school, I got As; I was a caregiver for my siblings and a leader in sports and youth group. Great accomplishments in many ways, but I also used them to outrun pain and feelings.

In college, I majored in ministry and landed an internship, which turned into a job at a large church. A year into my role, I experienced a serious conflict that had erupted in our ministry. After a difficult meeting, a senior leader asked me, "How do you feel about this?" I became silent and dumbfounded. "Feel?" I didn't know what to do with that question. I was twenty-three, and I had never really made an "I feel _____" statement.

I tried to fix myself through conferences, books, assessments, and head knowledge. But what I had was a heart problem. I stuffed my emotions, leading to exhaustion, emptiness, and almost complete burnout.

I had to take an inner journey, making myself weak and vulnerable to God and to others. I'm thankful that I reached out to a few trusted friends who walked with me through that desert. Today, I'm still learning this new way of relating, paying attention to the interior realm, and letting God reveal my identity apart from my performance.

God has taken me to deeper levels in my ongoing inner journey, a journey where I run toward pain and not away from it. But I'm more alive to God, others, and myself than ever before.

Tara is a strong, passionate leader. Her own journey into the desert has given her a vision for the church, a vision we can all resonate with. Here is the challenge before us — to become a community that welcomes those who want to own their journey by helping them develop relationships that nurture them toward growth and maturity. Tara puts it this way: "Imagine if the church became a community where people could truly be seen and known. A community where we could journey together. A place where we can take off masks and value authenticity more than performance. The best way to create this culture is to vulnerably lead by example. How much are you in tune with your own feelings? How do you value the feelings of others? Has God deeply transformed your heart or just your head?"

WHAT'S STIRRING?

1. Which aspects about "owning the journey" seem most appealing? Most difficult? Most important in the process of transformation?

2. How do you respond to the idea that "the Lord is your life"? In what way is that true for you today? What other sources of "life" or well-being do you tend to draw from?

3. Who, if anyone, has helped you experience a deeper life with God?

4. Read Psalm 139. What kind of circumstances do you imagine might have led someone to compose such a psalm?

5. Have you ever experienced a "desert" season? What led you into that season? Who, if anyone, accompanied or led you through it?

CHAPTER 4
BECOME A DESERT GUIDE

Desert guides do not shy away from someone else's "dark side." They fully understand that the inner journey takes courage and companionship, both of which can be hard to find when life is confusing. So rather than withdrawing or ignoring this season in others, these soul companions move *toward*, not away. One of the most compelling gifts a desert guide offers is empathy. Having been through the desert themselves, these individuals are hard-wired with compassion, grace, and a deep confidence that desert experiences hold the potential to produce great transformation.

ANTICIPATING THE JOURNEY

How do we develop the types of relationships needed to support this vital stage of spiritual growth? As we have seen, what growing followers of Christ most need at this stage is not more information but wise guides who can help them grow in their ability to discern and apply to their own experience the truths they have learned.

Individuals—and whole churches—can help by anticipating this necessary stage of spiritual formation. Beyond encouragement and companionship, desert guides also bring instruction and insight. As we have seen, growing followers of Christ are learning key spiritual practices and becoming acquainted with the contour lines of their own story. Ideally, the church could lead well in both areas, but interior journeying is harder to systematize than Learning Together ministry initiatives. It can be messy, and therefore it often gets pushed to the margins of a church organization. Sadly, though, our failure to expect and nurture this stage leads many to abandon the church as a source of help.

In her book *Community Is Messy*, Heather Zempel provides a great image of the challenge we face when leading people through this stage. Heather knows from her own experience in leading small groups at National Community Church in Washington DC that when the dark side comes out, it makes a royal mess. And it presents a decision for us as leaders. Heather puts it this way:

> Community is messy because it always involves people, and people are messy. It's about people hauling their brokenness and baggage into your house and dumping it in your living room.
>
> What do you do at that moment? The moment you realize that the people you've committed your life to are messy becomes the defining moment of your leadership.[1]

Rather than running from the mess or trying to fix the mess in unhelpful ways, we stay firmly committed to those in the Journeying Together stage. We must let them know they are welcome, just as they are, even as they express disappointments and frustration. In situations where severe brokenness may warrant professional help, leaders can still support this stage of growth by encouraging those doing deep soul work to remain connected. The point is, we should not be surprised—this stage should be expected.

A VISION FOR MESSY ENGAGEMENT

In this stage, leaders must be willing to wade into the mess of another person's life with God. They begin to do this by casting a fresh vision for the role of relationships in the spiritual growth process. This vision must take leaders beyond merely imparting information to cultivating a relationship of discernment. In his book *Your Church Is Too Safe*, pastor Mark Buchanan describes what this is like:

> When someone brings their mess into the light, their mess usually doesn't get cleaned up unless one of us wades into the mess with them. "Brothers and sisters," Paul writes to the Galatians, "if someone is caught in a sin, you who live by the Spirit should restore that person gently. But watch yourselves, or you also may be tempted. Carry each other's burdens, and in this way you will fulfill the law of Christ. If any of you think you are something when you are nothing, you deceive yourselves. Each of you should test your own actions. Then you can take pride in yourself, without comparing yourself to somebody else, for each of you should carry your own load" (Galatians 6:1–5 TNIV).
>
> This is a remarkable passage. The role of the mature — those "who live by the Spirit" — is to wade into another's mess, not to judge them or join them or feel superior to them or codependently take responsibility for them ("carry each other's burdens," Paul says, and then right after says "each of you should carry your own load"). The role of the mature is to wade into another's mess in order to "restore that person gently."[2]

By God's design, we have a role to play in carrying grace and truth into the mess of each other's lives. Our task is not to judge, commiserate with, or take responsibility for someone else's mistakes, but to restore. Senior leaders in the church are responsible for upholding this value and affirming that this way of relating is not only possible but essential if the church is to function in healthy, restorative ways.

SIGNS OF LIFE

A quick glance around the Arizona desert where my parents live may lead one to believe it is an environment devoid of life (except for the golf courses). Some of the places we hike look like the moon. You see nothing but rocks, dust, and dirt — until you take a closer look, that is. Stay still, get quiet — and you'll quickly learn that the desert is very much alive. My father, a scientist, always reminds me that appearances can be deceiving. Something may appear lifeless, but much can still be happening below the surface.

A spiritual desert may similarly appear to be dry, hostile, and barren, but it is actually a place that pulsates with life. That life is just hidden from view. In this stage, a person may feel, at a surface level, as if their life with God is bleak, unfruitful, and inhospitable. But there are almost always hidden signs of life—we just have to be quiet and still long enough to see them emerge. Sometimes it takes a wise and experienced guide to know just where to look.

In his book *A Hidden Wholeness*, Parker Palmer states, "Spaces designed to welcome the soul and support the inner journey are rare. But the principles and practices that shape such spaces are neither new nor untested." He continues with a powerful metaphor of the messy soul in community:

> Like a wild animal, the soul is tough, resilient, resourceful, savvy, and self-sufficient: it knows how to survive in hard places. I learned about these qualities during my bouts with depression. In that deadly darkness, the faculties I had always depended on collapsed. My intellect was useless; my emotions were dead; my will was impotent; my ego was shattered ...
>
> If we want to see a wild animal, the last thing we should do is go crashing through the woods yelling for it to come out. But if we will walk quietly into the woods, sit patiently at the base of a tree, breathe with the earth, and fade into our surroundings, the wild creature we seek might put in an appearance ...
>
> Unfortunately, *community* in our culture too often means a group of people who go crashing through the woods together, scaring the soul away.[3]

In our sincere zeal to help people grow, we often develop structures that fail to acknowledge or appreciate the inner journey—this second stage of spiritual growth. We aren't sure how to support those who are on this journey. But it doesn't have to be this way. Churches can adapt and expand their existing structures to better support those at this stage of spiritual growth.

Before we look at some of these changes, it is helpful to grasp clearly the signs of life in this stage. There are at least eight signs we can observe in the lives of those we guide:

1. *Acceptance of brokenness.* Acceptance does not mean people are glad for their brokenness; it does mean they no longer try to hide from it or deny it.

2. *Steady faith.* This is a simple confidence that God is still present, even in the mess and pain.

3. *Freedom from the past.* Those who are growing in this stage experience an increased freedom from shame and guilt when talking about their past.

4. *Growing dependence on God.* This is a growing awareness of their true identity in God while moving away from relying on themselves.

5. *Increased awareness of our need for God's grace.* This is a deeper awareness not only of their need for grace but also of how grace has a sustaining and transformative power in the here and now.

6. *Ability to recognize God's activity.* Growing disciples show an increased awareness of where God is at work, both within themselves and in the world around them.

7. *Yieldedness and obedience to God.* Beyond merely discerning God's guidance, conviction, or prompting, there is a willingness to take action and follow through.

8. *Growth in humility.* This translates into a willingness to serve others, especially without recognition, putting the needs and interests of others before their own.

As a leader, be on the lookout for these exciting signs of life in the people you lead. Use them to encourage by sharing where you see these things evident in their lives. The presence of these signs isn't meant to deny the reality of the desert, but it is an indication that there is progress and growth. Those who are growing will sense God's nearness and loving presence in the midst of their struggles. This sort of progress differs from the typical way we think of achievement, because it is a reflection of the soul's responsiveness to God's grace.

Along with these signs of life, the overall focus of growth in this stage is from desiring to attain *more knowledge about God* to simply wanting *more of God*. This can include knowledge, but it is not limited to that. You can begin to recognize it by listening to how someone speaks about their faith. In conversations, they begin to move from speaking about what they know of God to speaking more freely of their experience of God. We find a helpful illustration of this shift in the French language, which has two very different words for *knowing*. The verb *savoir* refers to facts—the realm of knowledge as information and data. The word *connaître*, however, is used to describe how we know another person—a relational form of knowledge.[4]

In guiding people through this stage, we must listen for both their *connaître* knowing and their *savoir* knowing—their experience *with* God as well as their ongoing knowledge *of* God. One way to do this is to ask questions that keep spiritual conversations centered on a person's actual relationship with God. When I'm helping someone in this stage, I want to affirm the transition they are making from knowing truths about God to having confidence in God, right here and right now. I listen for clues as to whether a person's life with God is based mostly on *facts and truths about* God or on their *experience of* God. Guiding in the Journeying Together stage involves both affirming the validity of those truths and pushing gently into the realm of their actual experience of God.

BALANCING DIRECTION AND DISCERNMENT

As mentioned earlier, this stage involves a shift from the more directive relationship of the first stage to a relationship that provides nearly equal parts of direction and discernment.

The focus of a leader's *direction* is on guiding a learning process through important concepts that will support this stage. Whether teaching about spiritual practices that support a person's life with

God or explaining the importance of one's story, the direction that a leader gives helps structure the journey. In contrast, the leader's *discernment* focuses on helping that individual learn by noticing and naming the spiritual dynamics going on inside and around them. Naturally, discernment can't be planned in advance or mass-produced.

Spiritual Transformation in Relationships

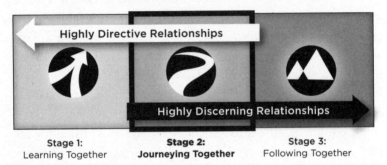

Stage 1:	Stage 2:	Stage 3:
Learning Together	Journeying Together	Following Together

Direction

Leaders provide guidance and structure by focusing their directive work on three primary goals:

1. Cultivate a safe relational environment.
2. Cultivate a strong spiritual environment.
3. Guide through an appropriate curriculum.

1. Cultivate a safe relational environment. It's impossible for people to take the risky step of looking beneath the surface of their lives if they feel uneasy, threatened, or fearful of being judged. Like the wild animal described earlier, most people will open up only if they are in an environment of relational trust and safety. Leaders need to create a caring community in which people carry one another to Jesus, much as the friends of the paralyzed man did in the gospels of Matthew, Mark, and Luke.

John Burke, pastor of Gateway Church in Austin, Texas, shares how he encourages his congregation to develop these types of relationships:

God loves to use ordinary people—just like you and me—to make each other healthy and whole as we run this race together. But it doesn't happen without giving lots of encouragement to each other—that's the soil in which God causes the growth. Without that kind of soil, people won't trust you to carry their mat, and you won't let them carry yours. Do a little self-assessment—how well do you do creating an encouraging environment for people close to you—one that helps them stay connected to God?[5]

The most effective leaders establish an environment that invites vulnerability and authenticity. Instead of ignoring or, worse, shaming those who share their brokenness, failures, and wounds, they welcome and receive these vulnerable admissions with grace, hope, truth, and encouragement.

2. Cultivate a strong spiritual environment. Leaders encourage awareness of God's presence—with us at all times and in all circumstances—by intentionally and routinely acknowledging God's activity in the midst of whatever else is going on. Though God may feel far-off when someone is overcome by anger, fear, despair, sadness, or confusion, leaders affirm that God remains near. We can imagine that the disciples on the road to Emmaus following Jesus' crucifixion knew what it was to experience anger, fear, despair, sadness, and confusion. They are lost in the discouragement and disillusionment of grief and dashed hopes. God is nowhere to be seen, at least from their limited perspective. They do not discern that Jesus—the incarnate Son of God—is right there, walking with them the entire time.

As he promised, Jesus is always with us as well, hidden but very present as we make the journey together. Like the disciples on the road to Emmaus, people in our churches may find themselves in despair, murmuring the words "But we had hoped ..." (Luke 24:21). Wise leaders help people recognize the presence of God, even in the midst of their discouragement and failed hopes.

How do we deliberately establish this kind of spiritual environment? It's not only through what we say; it is evidenced by our prayerful, quiet confidence in God as well. Sometimes the best thing we can do is listen, silently bathing in prayer our conversation and the desert dweller who is with us. What matters most is not the information a leader can impart but the understanding, acceptance, and simple trust that God's active presence and grace are at work in the situation.

3. *Guide through an appropriate curriculum.* You may be tempted to question the role of a curriculum in this stage of growth and formation. But a strong curriculum can raise important ideas and encourage thoughtful reflection while still freeing the leader to discern, observe, and deeply listen to God and others. Whether used with a group or simply to provide structure to a one-on-one relationship, the right curriculum can help facilitate the conversations that need to happen in this stage.

A Few Curriculum Possibilities

Excellent curriculum options exist. Some focus on learning core spiritual practices; others give insight on how to examine our past and embrace our story. Here are a few I've found helpful to guide and structure my relationships with people in the Journeying Together stage:

- Allender, Dan, *To Be Told: Know Your Story, Shape Your Future.*

  This book and the accompanying workbook are helpful for guiding readers to value, understand, and even to come to love their story in order to coauthor, with God, a new future.

- Soul Care Resources. Study guides include *Discovering Soul Care, Simplicity, Soul Searching,* and *Spiritual Friendship.*

  I've developed this series of resources to address some of the needs of those in this stage of growth.[6]

- Smith, James Bryan. *A Spiritual Formation Workbook: Small-Group Resources for Nurturing Christian Growth.*

This book uses the six "streams" of Christian experience throughout history to introduce core spiritual practices that reflect a balanced life with God.

- ———. The Apprentice Series. *The Good and Beautiful God*, *The Good and Beautiful Life*, and *The Good and Beautiful Community*. [7]

These books unpack life in the kingdom of God through helpful group curriculum and easy to follow soul-training exercises in each chapter.

- Wakefield, James L. *Sacred Listening: Discovering the Spiritual Exercises of Ignatius Loyola.*

The spiritual exercises of Saint Ignatius can provide an excellent format for spiritual growth during this stage. For a Protestant audience, James Wakefield has published a fantastic resource. Some will find it helpful to connect with Jesuit retreat centers for additional resources that draw from the rich background of the Catholic tradition.

Discernment

When we journey together with someone, we as leaders must both practice discernment and seek to develop discernment within the life of the person we are serving. We practice discernment by helping people learn how to recognize and talk about their experience with God. This is especially important when someone encounters resistance to healing, growth, or grace, or when they struggle with feelings of shame or trauma. Leaders can focus their discernment efforts in four helpful areas: (1) finding ways to connect a person's experiences to God's activity, (2) praying for inner healing, (3) looking for glimpses of God, and (4) identifying when a person is ready to move on.

1. Find ways to connect experiences to God's activity. Several years ago, I found myself weeping unexpectedly during a scene in a movie—a scene that wasn't particularly sad or moving. Afterward, a friend helped me realize I wasn't suffering from a case of malfunctioning tear ducts, but rather that God was using this experience to speak healing words I very much needed to hear. I wouldn't normally have made that connection or stopped to pay much attention to what was happening within my heart if my friend hadn't helped me connect my experience with God's activity. As we prayerfully listen to the stories people share with us, we need to be alert to the activity of God in the midst of daily life. Wise leaders will recognize when God is at work and will draw out these experiences for further prayer and reflection.

2. Pray for inner healing. When we journey with others in this stage, we get a front-row seat to the areas of their lives that need healing. So what do we do with what we see and learn? Sometimes the best thing we can do is pray with them and for them. Prayer is not the only thing we can do, but it should always be one of the primary ways we respond to people in their need for healing. We can pray silently on our own, or we can pray aloud in the presence of the other person. Either way, we need to pray.

Jesus' teaching on prayer in Luke 11 challenges me to do this on behalf of my friends. In the parable of the friend who asks to borrow food at midnight, Jesus reminds us that God is pleased with those who demonstrate boldness in their prayer requests. Applying the parable to prayer, Jesus commends courageous prayer and affirms God's willingness to listen and respond: "I tell you, even though he will not get up and give you the bread because of friendship, yet *because of your shameless audacity* he will surely get up and give you as much as you need" (Luke 11:8, emphasis added). I know I want to be marked by that kind of shameless audacity.

3. Look for glimpses of God in someone's history. For many of us, it's painful to talk about the past. Shame, whether deserved or undeserved, keeps us quiet. A gentle, discerning presence not only invites others to share their story but also helps them find glimpses of God in their past—glimpses they might otherwise have missed. Because we tend to reinforce what we already know and believe, an outside observer can sometimes notice something we don't see or have forgotten and can point out God's provision, protection, or guidance that was there for us during troubling times. Like the disciples on the road to Emmaus, we can be blind to the presence of Jesus until later in our journey with him. When we finally see him, we realize he was with us all along. Wise desert guides who listen well can sometimes discern what we cannot see, sensing the presence of God in our past when we felt most alone and abandoned.

4. Identify readiness to move on. As people move through the Journeying Together stage of spiritual growth, it's important to look for signs that a person is ready to move on—but now with a new foundation of greater strength. The Journeying Together stage of inner growth and healing has accomplished its goal—teaching and training a person to deeply depend on God in any and all circumstances, accept their own brokenness, and embrace their unique story of God's design. Pay particular attention to any unanticipated invitation at this stage. Though the inner journey continues for a lifetime (as does the process of learning), it may be time to move on. Look for signs that a person is ready to share with others the grace and wisdom they have learned. Are they ready to mentor? Are they ready to help others with their story?

FINDING THE RIGHT RELATIONAL FORMAT

For people in this stage, several helpful relational formats can be considered. In chapter 2, I discussed several relational formats (small groups, for example) that may be well-known to you. Because the Journeying Together stage is less familiar to many church leaders, I'll elaborate on several relational formats that are appropriate for this stage of spiritual growth.

Spiritual Formation Focused Small Group. We know that small groups can be helpful in the first stage of growth. Often, as people mature and grow, they find this format less helpful, but a shift in the group's focus can sometimes make a small group appropriate for this stage. As people are learning about the core spiritual disciplines, particularly for the first time, it can be useful to have a small group explore and practice core themes together. These might include learning about prayer, engaging at a more reflective level with Scripture, practicing spiritual friendship, or engaging in the disciplines of solitude and silence.

A group can meet for a short period of time, perhaps during a guided retreat experience, or it can meet regularly like any other small group. But the focus is unique—exploring new ways of caring for the soul and receiving sustenance and strength from God.

Spiritual Formation Class Experience. Similar to the small group format, the classroom experience is typically most useful in the first stage of growth—Learning Together. Many who are interested in growing more deeply in their faith will want a class experience that covers the basics of spiritual formation. This class will focus on the core spiritual disciplines and give opportunities for applying what is learned and talking about it with others in the class. A class should incorporate teaching, experience, reflection, discussion, and even homework assignments between sessions.

Troy's Story

Sometimes the ideas and experiences presented in a classroom environment can catapult someone to a new awareness of their dependence on God and lead to a willingness to take next steps. Troy is a friend and fellow minister who participated in some classes I taught recently. He shares some thoughts about the experience.

"When the pace of your life outstrips the health of your soul, eventually, predictably, you are headed for a crash."

I heard the words at my church as if I was watching a movie in slow motion. Simultaneously I heard another voice in my head saying simply, "Buckle up—because that's you."

I didn't know why I felt so tired and sick all the time. I didn't know why I was so anxious and sad. I didn't know what was missing, but I knew something was terribly wrong on the inside. I had plenty of knowledge about God and even ministry, but it was as if my soul was withering. I refused to listen to it;

the whole experience made no sense. So my body took over and got my attention, and finally I began to listen. I later came to see the fatigue and physical symptoms as a "blessed mutiny"— my body refused to go any farther under my leadership.

I had been a believer since a young age, gone to a Christian college, and worked in a successful role at a successful church. I was aware of my core wounds, my brokenness, and the masks I wore so people wouldn't see those parts of me. I was also becoming aware that self-knowledge and self-protection were not bringing healing. Some confusion and hopelessness began to settle in as I realized I was meandering in a very dry and thirsty land.

It was at this point that God led the ideas of soul care into my life through Mindy. She became my desert guide during her classes and over an occasional cup of coffee at Starbucks, as she pointed me toward this inner journey. I had gone through Christian counseling, and while that was very helpful, this was different. She challenged the presence of functional atheism in my life, even demonstrating it with a version of the classic bridge illustration that showed my tendency to assume that, while I was saved by God's grace, the rest of my life (beyond salvation) depended on me.

I began to learn that the Holy Spirit is available to walk with me through each moment if I will quiet the din of my life enough to hear him. My journey inward became a journey into the spiritual practices, which led me toward a deepening level of daily dependence. I got back into therapy and found a spiritual director, and I experienced some of the healing I had always believed was possible. God used Mindy—both the things she said and the way she said them—to change my life from the inside out, and it's only just begun.

What began in a classroom as a series of casual conversations eventually moved to a coffee shop, where Troy shared several desert experiences and took steps to engage in his inner journey of growth.

Spiritual Friendship. Spiritual friendship is an intimate, life-giving relationship where people pay attention and are responsive to the activity of God in their lives. This intentional attentiveness to God opens us up to deeper transformation.

Sometimes the concept of spiritual friendships is erroneously relegated to the "pink zone." But it is far more accurate to view them from a kingdom perspective, where the participants come figuratively dressed in battle fatigues, ready to fight for one another's growth and freedom. David and Jonathan are a good example of a spiritual friendship—would-be rivals caring for, encouraging, and sacrificing for one another.

In a spiritual friendship, the relationship is based on mutual sharing and growth. Though there may be times when one person shares more than another or is in greater need of encouragement, prayer, and support, spiritual friendships are relationships among peers who are growing and seeking God together.

Spiritual Direction. Though they can appear similar at times, a relationship of spiritual direction differs from a spiritual friendship in that one individual, the director, is primarily focused on helping the directee. These relationships are not as mutual as a spiritual friendship, though a director and directee may still be friends. In relationships of spiritual direction, the nature of the relationship may shift from time to time as needed, occasionally focusing more intentionally on specific areas of growth.

Several distinct approaches to spiritual direction exist, each with slightly different goals. In the classical approach to spiritual direction, the director meets with the directee to expand the directee's experience of God in prayer. While this may seem like a narrow focus, the classical approach is rooted in the belief that increasing a directee's experience of God directly through prayer will necessarily increase their experience of God. This approach is somewhat similar to the work a marriage counselor does to improve communication between a husband and wife. Improving the capacity for communication improves everything else. Of course, in this case the problem is not an error in God's communication to us—the problem is in our ability to hear, understand, and respond to him. A spiritual director helps us learn how to pray and communicate with God.

In addition to the classical prayer-focused approach to spiritual direction, some spiritual directors embrace a more therapeutic approach. In this case, spiritual direction, while not a replacement for traditional psychotherapy or counseling, does include the use of psychological principles. Larry Crabb defines this approach to spiritual direction as "the process of exploring and understanding the interior world of another person, recognizing both the work of the flesh and the work of the Spirit, and following the Spirit's work in transforming the person's interior world to become more like Christ."[8]

I've personally benefited from directors who have employed both of these approaches, as well as from some who use a hybrid approach that combines prayer with therapeutic principles. Whatever approach is used, a spiritual director can be a trustworthy guide for a person who is learning to navigate the inner world of their heart. Directors provide a safe and structured environment for growth at this stage of maturity.

Counseling. In some circumstances, a person who wishes to grow through this stage will benefit most from the assistance of a trained counselor or therapist. Though many will find healing and hope through a wise spiritual director, there are sometimes deeper wounds or traumatic experiences that are best supported by those who can offer additional guidance through their areas of expertise. Yet even when a trained counselor is sought for help, it is the ordinary relationships in a person's life that greatly aid their ability to embrace the healing they experience. Counseling helps us own our story, and sometimes we need the wise guidance of a trained professional to understand the past, gain insight into what is actually going on deep within us, and then move forward in our journey.

Though counseling may seem similar to spiritual direction, it differs in a few ways. One difference is the type of training. Spiritual directors can be formally trained in a variety of ways, but some may have no training at all but simply be gifted persons who use their gifts in the body of Christ. A trained therapist, on the other hand, is licensed and subject to a different set of accountabilities and professional standards. Notably, the fee structures for counseling are usually quite different from those for spiritual direction.

Another difference is also significant and worth consideration. While counselors may choose to incorporate the spiritual dimension into their meeting times, this is the intentional and deliberate focus of a spiritual director. Spiritual directors will certainly consider other areas of life as well, but the focal point of the time together is God and a person's experience of God. Trained counselors may choose to spend their time focusing on family relationships or other areas from a person's past and may not typically have the same God-centered focus a spiritual director has. Both types of relationships are helpful and, at times, necessary.

Twelve-Step Recovery Groups. Twelve-step recovery groups are relational formats that help people break free from self-destructive lifestyles. These groups are particularly meaningful to Christ followers when the twelve not-so-simple steps are deeply anchored in biblical truth. The twelve steps work, not because they are a magic formula for transformation, but because they reorient people to a right relationship with God, self, and others.

Those who work the twelve steps begin by admitting *they need help.* Denial is no longer an option. Many describe this turning point — when they were finally forced to face their addiction — as "hitting bottom." Others more positively refer to it as "the gift of desperation." The mark of this stage of growth is a growing aware-ness of our dependence on and need for God. The truth is that all of us, given our very real and ongoing need for God — can be similarly blessed by any circumstance that enables us to receive this gift of desperation. For some, this is the fallout of an addictive lifestyle, and involvement in a twelve-step group is the relational format God uses to bring healing and hope. Sometimes it's only possible to "go there" — to tolerate the pain of hitting bottom and facing the dark-ness — when we believe there are *relationships* where people will catch us when we land.

Many churches and civic organizations have opened their doors — or more often than not, their basements — to these leaderless gatherings of people who are committed to working a transformative process together. I've occasionally heard those in recovery groups question the lack of a similar level of commitment to transformation among those in the church. "Why is it that those who go to the basement of the church get better, and those who stay upstairs never do?" There may be more truth to this question than we care to admit.

Intensive Retreat Experiences. Though this last example is not a relational format, it is worth mentioning, since it often leads to significant breakthroughs in the growth and maturity process. An intensive retreat experience can be a time away from the typical hustle and bustle of life, a break in the routines that brings rest and fresh perspective. When we take a step back from life, we can gain some physical, emotional, and psychological distance from our current circumstances. To do so often allows space for growth to occur. Because many of these intense experiences deal with deep issues from our past, typically they are gender-specific, serving either men or women.

A retreat of this kind is best seen as a "turning point" opportunity, something that connects a person with the necessary resources and relationships that can offer long-term support for the rest of the journey. The experience itself should not become the focus; rather it should serve as a stepping-stone to another relational format — a spiritual formation group, a spiritual friendship, a relationship of spiritual direction, or simply a small group focused on the same issue.

FINDING THE RIGHT LEADERS

Leaders who guide others in this stage need to be ready to meet people in their brokenness, disillusionment, and doubt by offering them companionship and care — not simplistic answers or shaming criticisms. It is best if leaders have been through their own desert experience. Just as no one but a sober, recovering alcoholic can sponsor someone through recovery in the twelve steps, only someone who has truly been through the disorientation and desperation of their own inner journey can effectively walk with someone else during this time.

See the table below for several important leadership qualities and spiritual gifts as you seek to identify effective desert guides for those in the Journeying Together stage of growth:

Leadership Qualities	Spiritual Gifts
• Familiarity with the purpose and practice of spiritual disciplines that are helpful to this stage and confidence in explaining them to others • Ability to create a safe and trusting relational environment that invites vulnerability • Ability to recognize the signs of God's activity and presence in the lives of others • Skill in discerning the locus of dependency—relative trust in God or self—in those they are guiding • Ability to notice what's going on inside themselves as they listen to someone else • Confident belief and trust in God's ongoing work in another's life • Willingness and ability to be a prayerful presence for others, whether or not one is physically present with them	• Teaching • Shepherding • Encouragement • Leadership • Discernment • Mercy

The kind of people who can lead others through this stage of the journey are skilled in offering both discernment and direction. They maintain a clear vision of the purpose of this stage, which is owning the journey. A variety of spiritual gifts can beautifully support this process, each in their own way.

As you look at the list of leadership qualities, you may recognize these in yourself or in those who have helped you in your journey. And the good news is that all of these qualities can be cultivated. No advanced degree is required, just careful attentiveness to the ongoing activity of God in another person, with the willingness to provide guidance as needed.

Leaders who accompany others in this stage need to refrain from offering quick-exit strategies or easy "answers," even when those in pain are very much looking for answers! Wise leaders focus on being a loving presence — someone who won't run away in the face of sin, darkness, failure. They listen, invite self-disclosure, share their own story, and ultimately help those they guide to discover God's story at work in the midst of their own.

While it may seem obvious, we must remember that a willingness to pray with and for someone as they journey through this stage is essential. At the end of the day, there is only so much any one human being can do on behalf of another. But in prayer, we invite God's power to have full sway in the unseen places. This is no small thing; even deeply submerged mountains can be moved.

Five Questions for Leaders

1. In what ways, if any, are you sensing God's presence these days?
2. In what circumstances is it most difficult to sense God's presence or goodness?
3. What helps you meaningfully connect with God?
4. What is the general feeling you have about prayer these days? Why?
5. Where are you feeling stuck in your relationship with God?

A CHURCH THAT EXPECTS THE INNER JOURNEY

You may read through the list of relational formats for this stage and realize that your ministry environment doesn't have any of these options in place. You may wonder whether any churches are really stepping up to address the needs of people in this Journeying Together stage, and if they are, what are they doing?

Christ Church of Oak Brook, Illinois, led by Pastor Dan Meyer and his team, is a great example of a church that intentionally focuses on the relational needs of people on the pathway toward spiritual maturity. The team at Christ Church has arranged their entire ministry to relationally support those who are going through their spiritual journeys, with particular attention given to the needs of people at this second stage of growth. The acronym STEP describes their focus on spiritual growth for all members of the community.

S = **Sight** for the pathway. How do I chart my spiritual journey?

T = **Training** for the soul. How do I connect with God between Sundays?

E = **Equipment** for life. What can I learn about better daily living?

P = **Partners** for the journey. Who are the companions I need to keep growing?

Leaders throughout the church embody this process — living it out themselves — and are trained to skillfully offer spiritual companionship to others. All who attend the church are welcome to participate, and everyone is challenged to take a next step toward growth.

To offer particular aid to those who are in the second stage of spiritual growth — the Journeying Together stage — the congregation makes spiritual direction services available to members.[9] In other words, at Christ Church, it's entirely normal for a person to see a spiritual director. Those who want to take the necessary steps of looking inward and developing habits and patterns of spiritual disciplines can find someone who has traveled the path before, a desert guide who can offer counsel and direction.

WHAT IF PEOPLE DON'T MOVE ON?

In every stage of spiritual growth, there is the potential to get stuck. Getting stuck in the second stage is a bit different from getting stuck in the Learning Together stage, but it's still possible, and it's still tragic when people give up on deeper growth and change. There are at least three ways people can get stuck in this stage: in their pain, in escapism, or in timidity.

Stuck in Pain

We get stuck in our pain when we choose to remain a victim rather than taking responsibility for our future. In my own life, I've held on at times to my victimized status because it protected me from the risks required to move forward. It was more comforting to stay stuck when I could blame my inactivity on someone who had wronged me. But at some point, all of us who are stuck have to acknowledge that, even if what happened wasn't our fault, we have to answer the question, *Now what?*

When I was stuck in this way, I heard an analogy that shocked me into action. A speaker asked us, "What would you do if you were out jogging and got hit by a car?" Would you lie by the side of the road lamenting your pain because the accident wasn't your fault? Would you allow your broken leg to define the rest of your life? Not likely. Most of us would seek help. We would seek healing so we could return to our lives again. So why do we choose to wallow in the wounded places in our past, allowing the damage of relationships from long ago to define the way we live?

Getting stuck in our pain is quite different from experiencing and owning our pain. When you encounter someone trapped in this way, you need to love them enough to ask about it. Mirror back to them what you observe, gently pointing out what you see. "I notice that you keep focusing on this, but rather than seeing it as part of your history, it seems like you're beginning to let it define you or determine your future. Is this something you notice as well?" It may take time and patience to pull a person out of their pain, but gentle prodding and a commitment to speaking the truth can help draw their attention beyond past hurts at the right time, in order to focus on God's future.

Stuck in Escapism

Another way in which people get stuck is by using spiritual practices not as a way of moving forward but as an excuse to disengage and do nothing. As a "spiritual formation person" (yes, some people do call me that), people expect me to promote all things related to spiritual practices without hesitation — things like journaling, solitude, silence, and the like. But I do not always and in every circumstance advocate these things. While disciplines and practices are helpful tools, we need to remember that they are only means to an end.

Over the years, I have noticed a tendency in myself and in others to use spiritual practices as an excuse to withdraw from the pain and complexity of life. *I'm not having that hard conversation because I need a few weeks/months/years to journal about it. I'm not making that difficult decision today because I need to spend the day in solitude praying about it.* Sometimes it is good and necessary to pursue a spiritual practice that will help us make a centered decision or surrender to God in a specific way. But it is also possible to use spiritual activity to avoid making decisions, to avoid facing difficult relationships, and to even justify our own unwillingness to change. It takes great discernment to recognize this because it often happens to those who appear to be spiritually mature and healthy. Sadly, this form of self-deception can be lethal if not confronted.

I know of an entire ministry team that, with good intentions, chose to spend a year focusing their efforts on just "being" rather than on the "doing" side of their ministry. After a year of this, the person who oversaw that team confided in me: "They sit around the same candle every week, and nothing whatsoever has changed in their lives or in the lives of those they are called to serve." In their effort to seek maturity, they had somehow stopped growing. To be fair, I don't know all the details of this situation, so there may have been other reasons for their inaction. But I hear the concern of the pastor overseeing the team, and I suspect that at some level they were using their spiritual activities as an excuse to avoid the hard work of doing ministry.

The race God calls us to run includes seasons of engagement and disengagement. Both are important. For most of us, while we need to step back from our work and ministry from time to time, what we really need is a rhythm of life that is flexible. We should never use the pursuit of a deeper walk with God or our engagement in spiritual disciplines as an excuse to avoid the work of facing our past and our ongoing responsibilities. As we are formed into the image of Christ, the goal of our transformation, we will gain strength and courage to face our lives and our relationships.

Ancient and modern spiritual masters affirm that, when rightly pursued, our contemplation and our activities possess a strong and natural correlation. Practices of withdrawal should draw us deeply into the heart of God, and as we grow closer to the heart of God, we naturally should be drawn deeper into the needs of the world. If anything, our sense of powerlessness in fixing the problems of the world should reveal to us just how deeply we need God. Engagement in the reality of a sinful world leads us to retreat to the heart of God, which empowers us to return and engage in the needs of the world around us. It is a rhythm of engagement and withdrawal that leads us onward toward growth and maturity as we learn to depend on God and not ourselves. This constant shifting shows the natural ebb and flow of a spiritual life engaged with God in this very real world.

Stuck in Timidity

The most common way for people to get stuck, and the one with which I am most familiar, is through timidity—when we suffer from a lack of confidence and courage. Change is almost always scary, even when it's change for the better. Though a person may be taking steps to grow, learning how to face their brokenness and remain open to the grace and power of God, they haven't yet learned how to proceed with strength and authority. A person can sense God leading them but remain timid and hesitant, lacking boldness to step forward in faith.

Getting stuck in this way—failing to move ahead in faith and courage—bears some similarity to the story of the Israelites as they leave Egypt and prepare to enter the Promised Land. Before entering the land, Moses sent twelve spies to scout the enemy territory. Ten of them came back with a frightening report: "We can't attack those people; they are stronger than we are" (Numbers 13:31). Only two of the spies—Joshua and Caleb—refused to be timid. They saw the same things as the others, but they were ready to step forward in faith, trusting that God was leading them to a new place:

> "The land we passed through and explored is exceedingly good. If the LORD is pleased with us, he will lead us into that land, a land flowing with milk and honey, and will give it to us. Only do not rebel against the LORD. And do not be afraid of the people of the land, because we will devour them. Their protection is gone, but the LORD is with us. Do not be afraid of them."
>
> — Numbers 14:7–9

Their words are marked by humility and reveal a deep attitude of dependence—utter dependence, in fact—on God. Their confidence is not based on their own ability or superiority; it rests on two things: (1) God has commanded them to do this, and (2) God is their leader and protector.

I am grateful for wise friends and leaders who have called me to step out beyond my timidity and fear and have encouraged me to risk running the race I am called to run. I've spent time in the desert on the inner journey of transformation, but I've also come to see that not all of life is meant to be lived there. There comes a time to overcome our timidity, leave the desert, and take back the land.

HITTING BOTTOM AND MOVING ON

Leaders, mentors, friends, and pastors provide critical discernment for growing disciples in the Journeying Together stage. But the eventual goal is to leave this stage, though the practices and disciplines learned during this time will continue to nurture and strengthen healthy relationships with God and others. The goal is to move on to the next stage of spiritual growth, learning to follow Jesus together.

As we have seen, relationships are essential to this second stage of growth, and without them many people never move beyond but stay inwardly focused and isolated from healthy community. Henri Nouwen describes how he allowed himself to hit bottom *only* when his soul knew he was surrounded by safe and loving relationships. In *The Inner Voice of Love*, he describes his experience in language all of us can relate to:

> That was a time of extreme anguish, during which I wondered whether I would be able to hold on to my life. Everything came crashing down — my self-esteem, my energy to live and work, my sense of being loved, my hope for healing, my trust in God ... everything. Here I was, a writer about the spiritual life, known as someone who loves God and gives hope to people, flat on the ground and in total darkness.
>
> What had happened? I had come face to face with my own nothingness. It was as if all that had given my life meaning was pulled away and I could see nothing in front of me but a bottomless abyss.
>
> The strange thing was that this happened shortly after I had found my true home. After many years of life in universities, where I never felt fully at home, I had become a member of L'Arche, a community of men and women with mental disabilities. I had been received with open arms, given all the attention and affection I could ever hope for, and offered a safe and loving place to grow spiritually as well as emotionally. Everything seemed ideal. But precisely at that time I fell apart — as if I needed a safe place to hit bottom![10]

Perhaps, Nouwen suggests, those who begin this stage of growth — the inward spiritual journey — can somehow sense they have been offered "a safe place to hit bottom." Nouwen's experience is not unique to him. Occasionally you may hear someone describe a process of "hitting bottom," or you may discern them relating how God has met them in their weakness and notice they have been given the gift of desperation. It might be that God has placed you in their life because they are ready for a new season of growth.

Just remember that it is never the responsibility of a desert guide to solve anything. God has arranged the body of Christ to be a healing environment in which God, the Great Physician, does what only God can do. We simply help each other stay on the operating table as God works.

WHAT'S STIRRING?

1. Have you ever walked through a desert place with anyone? What did you bring to that relationship that was
   helpful?

2. What did you learn about the desert by helping someone else?

3. How much vision for this stage of spiritual development is present in your ministry? What helps reinforce
   that vision, and what detracts from that vision?

PART 3
FOLLOWING TOGETHER

CHAPTER 5
STAY THE COURSE

Leaving the desert is a wonderful feeling. From this seemingly barren wilderness, the soul emerges with a great harvest—a newfound depth of acceptance, peace, and an abiding joy in God. Perhaps the greatest fruit of the desert, ironically, is the resulting contentment—a profound grasp of the sufficiency of God's grace and love. It is a deep sense of being fundamentally well, of knowing with great certainty that "the LORD is my Shepherd, I lack nothing" (Psalm 23:1). I may still lack a thing or two in my day-to-day existence, of course, but I can celebrate the fact that I am under the watchful care of a good God.

As I step out of the desert and into the next stage of growth, I now understand my story, or at least I have a firm grasp of some of its major themes. I am no longer pridefully shocked by my sin and failures, nor am I desperate to hide my sin from those close to me. I know I have a role in God's purposes, and I am eager to participate in them. My motivation to change and act comes from a steadfast resolve to love God and do God's will, not from my own striving or ego. Following God feels different.

The peace that was once found primarily in withdrawal from the world is now experienced through engagement with the world. There are still areas of struggle and resistance to God, and I still deal with emotions like fear and anger. But there is now a strong foundation and the tested experience and discipline of the inner journey. A disciple in this stage is more comfortable with the uncomfortable, willing to look at herself in the mirror to discern hurtful patterns and face the truth. A disciple is familiar with some of the classic spiritual practices and a few of them have become natural and normal habits that help him stay connected to God, even (and especially) in hard times.

Those who enter this final stage of spiritual growth, the Following Together stage, face a unique challenge—staying the course and finishing the race. In this stage, while learning is an ongoing aspect of growth, life itself has become the curriculum. While there is continued growth inward, learning to face my sin, failure, and brokenness, I am now ready to minister to others in need as well. I am equipped to discern the deeper work of God within me while also discerning the activity of God around me. When I sense the Spirit move, I'm ready to follow—at any cost, and with joy.

REALLY?

One Christmas morning several years ago, I sat holding a gift handed to me by my husband. I spent several moments trying to guess what was in the heavy box. I had no idea. Was it a squishy book? A new Bible? Jeff watched eagerly as I unwrapped the mystery gift. His eyes told me he *knew* I'd love it.

But after tearing through the final layer of wrapping paper, I felt my heart sink. I held in my hands a lovely—and very expensive—leather-bound Day-Timer.* Anyone would have been thrilled to have it—it was the best of the best. But I was not one of those people. Instead, I was afraid.

---

*If you're under the age of thirty, you likely don't remember these! In the days before everything was stored electronically on our small devices, people used old-fashioned pens and paper in a notebook system to stay organized.

Perhaps you can guess why. You see, I had been learning to deeply distrust the many complicated sources that fueled my striving for success, to stay away from anything that promised me a "highly effective" life. In the desert, I had learned to long for God, to find my contentment in him. I had discovered a God who did not use me, but who loved me—a God who was very active in this world and who drew me into a deeper engagement with the world as I followed him. I had spent years disengaging from the achievement-oriented lifestyle, so when I saw that beautiful leather notebook, I felt like a recovering alcoholic, barely a few years sober, who'd been given a one-year membership to the wine-of-the-month club. What do you say to the gift giver in that situation? "Um, thanks"?

Of course, I did thank my husband. Not only for the gift, but for the vote of confidence it represented. Jeff had discerned that I was farther along on my journey than I even realized. He felt I was ready to move ahead and reengage with God's call on my life by stepping into the next season of life and ministry. Even today, my close friends will tell you I struggle to balance my aptitude for strategic thinking and planning with my desire to surrender, yield, and trust. Because my personal weaknesses lead me toward striving and achieving, I suspect I will always struggle to trust God in reengaging those gifts. But that's not an excuse to avoid them entirely. They represent my growth edge—a place in my life where God isn't finished working.

GOALS OF THE FOLLOWING TOGETHER STAGE

As we grow to maturity in Christ, our goal is to run with perseverance and be ready to throw off anything that gets in the way of that unique race God has marked out for us. Consider again the instruction from the writer of Hebrews:

> Therefore, since we are surrounded by such a great cloud of witnesses, let us throw off everything that hinders and the sin that so easily entangles. And let us run with perseverance the race marked out for us, fixing our eyes on Jesus, the pioneer and perfecter of faith. For the joy set before him he endured the

cross, scorning its shame, and sat down at the right hand of the throne of God. Consider him who endured such opposition from sinners, so that you will not grow weary and lose heart.

— Hebrews 12:1 – 3

As we have seen, at every stage of growth we need running mates who run beside us. Now, in this final stage, we need companions who will help us stay the course in at least three key areas: (1) cultivating ongoing awareness of the inner journey, (2) practicing ongoing abandonment to God's purposes, and (3) staying connected to others. These will serve as our goals of the Following Together stage of spiritual growth.

Cultivating Ongoing Awareness of the Inner Journey

Driving home from work one day, I realized I was angry and aggravated about a brief but upsetting conversation I'd had earlier that day. Without realizing it, the other person had touched on some painful places in my own life and story. But this person's lack of awareness about how I'd been hurt only made me more irritated and annoyed!

Now I was not only agitated but also mad at *how* agitated I was. I knew I was in an ugly place and that the only path out of this mess would be bringing it into the light. So I called a friend who knows me and would understand why I reacted the way I did. But I also knew she could gently bear witness to my dark side without indulging my grudge. After listening, empathizing, and pointing to glimpses of God's grace in the mess, she prayed for me — right there, over the phone.

I don't remember the outcome of that particular conflict, but I do remember the gift of having someone to turn to. I turned toward her and asked for help. I did not necessarily need instruction on what the Bible says about checking the attitude of my heart or loving my enemies. I also didn't need someone to help me rediscover the hidden places of pain and brokenness in my heart. All of those things are important and have their place, but in that moment, the Mindy who was struggling to run the race marked out for her needed someone who knew those things — and also knew I knew all those things—and could help me with the challenge of following Jesus on this particular day. I needed someone who could help me pay attention to my inner journey.

In this situation, several spiritual practices played an important role in helping me discern what was happening inside me. For example, soul-searching (my awareness that something wasn't right), confession (bringing my anger into the light of a relationship), extending grace (my friend's noticing God's hidden activity), and prayer were all instrumental in working through my anger. And the decision to share an everyday struggle with a friend was not a rare or unusual thing for me. It was just normal—a natural and expected part of throwing off whatever hinders and the sin that so easily entangles. It is not a one-time effort but a lifelong process, and it is something we can't do alone.

Practicing Ongoing Abandonment to God's Purposes

Rarely do we know in advance what God intends to do through us as we are transformed by his grace and love. We simply follow. And as we abandon ourselves to him, we become open to God's purposes in each circumstance of life we encounter.

Gary Haugen serves as president and CEO of International Justice Mission, which he founded in 1997. Gary and his staff of over five hundred professionals labor tirelessly in some of the darkest cities and regions of the world for the needs of those who have been denied justice. Their global mission: to rescue thousands, protect millions, and prove that justice for the poor is possible. Now that's a *vision*!

As a devoted Christ follower, Gary is clear on the fact that God is doing this work, not only through IJM staff, but from within IJM staff. In his view, "Leaders lead out of who they are on the *inside*. God does his miracles of transformation through miraculously *transformed* people."[1] I resonate deeply with this idea.

In his book *The Barbarian Way*, pastor Erwin McManus gives a compelling description of what can happen when we abandon ourselves to God:

> Just do whatever Jesus calls you to do the moment it is clear to you. Do not procrastinate; do not hesitate; do not deviate from whatever

course of action he calls you to … The more you trust him, the more you'll risk on his behalf. The more you love him, the more you will love others … Your expectations of Jesus will change as your intimacy with him deepens … We look to Jesus not to fulfill our shallow longings or to provide for us creature comforts. We look to him to lead us where he needs us most and where we can accomplish the most good.[2]

From this posture of surrender, we leave behind anything that might be considered our own agenda. We increasingly see the circumstances and people around us from God's eternal perspective. As we yield our lives more fully to God, we freely take risks for the sake of the kingdom. We now make ourselves — our stories and unique design — freely available to the needs of the world around us. In *To Be Told*, Dan Allender explains this vital connection between our stories and our service:

> To tell stories to impress or intimidate is to entrap — the opposite of telling stories to set others free. A gift-giving, liberating story tells of innocence lost, tragedy encountered, imagination employed, and the brief and glorious moments of an ending that reminds us again that our story is not finally written by us, but we coauthor it with God. The gift of this kind of story is the deep and fundamental reminder that we are not our own; we are God's. We invest in another when we see ourselves as uniquely privileged and available to join his or her story …
>
> Further, not to be cluttered with oneself is to embrace enough of our story to say to God and to others, "He is good. And he has written me well." And perhaps even more, being uncluttered calls me to wrestle with those stories that confuse me, the stories I continue to hold at arm's length. We will never be fully at ease with our story, but we can come to love our story profoundly and with more joy. Finally, to be uncluttered is to offer all of who we are, even the parts that are still unredeemed, for the redemption of others.[3]

Toward the end of his life, the apostle Paul confidently asserted, "I am already being poured out like a drink offering, and the time for my departure is near. I have fought the good fight, I have finished the race, I have kept the faith" (2 Timothy 4:6–7). The ultimate mark of following Jesus is a life poured out for the sake of others, like a drink offering. We live as Jesus would—deeply connected to God as our source of life, yet fully available to serve and give when asked to by God.

Staying Connected to Others

In order to best live on the fiery, glowing edge of what God has for us at any given moment, we must run our race *with others*. Without community, we will likely turn inward, and it won't be healthy or good for us. For some who have learned the value of withdrawal from the world and have tasted the fruit of the inward journey, there is a temptation to remain withdrawn. Others, to avoid the danger of burnout, perpetually say no to carrying burdens and getting involved in the lives of others. Neither extreme represents maturity.

> "God also creates a story with each person's life—a story that we are meant to tell. And since we are called to tell our story, we are also called to listen to the stories of others. And since we are to tell and to listen, then even more so we are called to encourage others to know and tell and listen to God's story as well as their own."
>
> **Dan Allender, *To Be Told***

Mark's Story

Sometimes we get so involved in serving the needs of others we forget our own need for the life-giving relationships that sustain us. That's what happened to my friend Mark Buchanan. Mark told me about his experience, using an illustration from the movie *The Lion King*:

> *In The Lion King, Simba—a self-obsessed, self-pitying young lion—loses his way after a tragic mistake. He wills a deep forgetfulness, rejecting who he is, spurning what he's called to. The pain of his past and the burden of his future are crushing. He avoids it all by throwing himself into a life of idleness and indulgence.*

It's so much fun, until it's not.

One day Simba meets Rafiki, a mandrill, a blue-faced baboon. Rafiki sits atop a branch and sings a nonsense song, half taunt, half ditty. Then he says to Simba, "I know who you are."

The chase is on. Rafiki swings from tree to tree, scrambles through thickets, darts and weaves, vanishes and appears. Simba gallops to catch him. At a turn in the chase, Rafiki says to Simba, "You are more than who you have become."

At last, Simba comes upon Rafiki by a pool in the forest. "I know who you are," Rafiki says again. "You are Mufasa's son." Mufasa was Simba's father. Mufasa was the Lion King. "Look," Rafiki says, and invites Simba to gaze at his own reflection in the pool. But all Simba sees is his own face.

"It's only me," he says, dejected.

"No," Rafiki says. "Look again." He drops a stone in the water. The surface ripples, then stills. And Simba sees, reflected in his own face, the face of his father. The face of the Lion King.

He rises, and runs straight into his destiny.

In Swahili, Mufasa means king.

Simba means lion.

Rafiki? That means friend.

A rafiki helps us see the Father's face reflected in our own. He helps us discover that we are more than who we have become. He helps us, despite our failures, despite our inadequacies, despite our fears, rise to our true self, take hold of our true calling.

I woke up one day, over a decade ago now, and realized I didn't have one, a rafiki.

I had just turned forty. I was enjoying life immensely. But I was friendless. There was not one person in my growing list of acquaintances and colleagues whom I would trust with the deep stuff. Not one I could call at 3:00 in the morning if my life was derailing. Not one I could call at 3:00 in the afternoon just to hang out.

So I went in search of a rafiki, and found a few. I had to take risks. I had to be vulnerable. I had to become curious. I had to drop my guard. I had to invite my rafikis to hold a mirror up to me, so I could see who I really was. So I could see who I might become.

And they held it, and I saw. I still have miles to go, but I see more clearly than ever the Father's face reflected in my own.

Such good rafikis.

Mark recognized the vital role that community plays in shaping his own soul and how much he needs other people to help him stay the course. Admittedly, deep friendships among those in vocational ministry leadership can be tricky. But those who make it for the long haul usually do so because they have a few good, close friends.

RELATIONSHIPS: KEY FOR THE JOURNEY AHEAD

For those in the Following Together stage, the relationships that help them continue pursuing God have a very different structure from that of the traditional small group or discipleship relationship. Some continue to meet with a spiritual director; others seek out the wisdom of a professional counselor. But for most people in this stage, the core relationships that nurture spiritual growth and health are peer-to-peer friendships with other Christ followers.

I have two sets of women who are companions on the journey right now. One of these groups gets together in person occasionally, but we remain in frequent contact through e-mail and phone for prayer support. The other group meets monthly. We have a clear purpose: to explore the edges of our lives, listening to what God is calling us to do and evaluating how we are responding and where we are stuck. In this group, there is no formal curriculum, but our relationships flourish due to high levels of discernment both offered and received. For example, I might talk about a book I am reading. Another woman in the group is reading some soul-stirring poetry, and still another is reading for her PhD program. One member of the group has just returned, exhausted and exhilarated, from an international ministry trip, and another is eyeball-deep in the challenges of parenting her energetic five-year-old.

At any given gathering, our conversation jumps from one deep topic to another as we laugh and challenge each other. But there is a method to our madness. We are listening deeply for the whispers of God in each other's lives. We are observing and discerning and affirming and questioning. We have high levels of trust—in God and in each other. Our exchanges are marked by deep honesty, so it's not unusual for blunt confessions to periodically tumble into the conversation. So, for example, when I share a frustration or struggle, my friends will mirror back to me what they've heard. They ask open-ended questions or draw my attention to things I may have missed—agitation, strengths, conviction, or sadness. My friends are examples of the kind of woman I want to be too—deeply trusting, attuned to God, and selflessly immersed in God's action around the world.

Each of us is also involved in the spiritual nurture and development of those who are not as far along on the journey. We mentor younger believers who are still just learning or taking steps to engage the inward journey, and this remains an important focus of our ministry. But I add this as a secondary focus, because many assume that mentoring younger believers is the only goal of this level of maturity. Some may wonder whether it is selfish to pursue mutual relationships that keep us focused on our own ongoing growth. Shouldn't we be entirely invested at this point in the building of less mature believers?

We may realize this is a false dichotomy, but it's worth stating it plainly. This is not an either-or proposition. Yes, these mature believers build into others. Their influence draws many into their sphere, and they have much to offer them. But mature believers will be significantly challenged by their peers through relationships that continue to "spur one another on," as the author of Hebrews challenges us, "toward love and good deeds" (Hebrews 10:24).

JOINING GOD IN HIS WORK

We cannot run unless we have first learned to walk. In the same way, we cannot move into the deepest levels of participation with God unless our souls have matured to the point where God can use us in this way. Author Dallas Willard describes this stage of the maturity process as moving "from surrender to drama." In other words, over time, we allow our will to become so absorbed into God's will that we become directly involved in the amazing drama of God's activity around us. Willard identifies a four-part developmental process that makes this possible: *surrender, abandonment, contentment*, and *participation*.[4] In describing these stages, I want to highlight the interior work that is needed for us to become *the kind of people* who can do those things that God might call us to do.

Surrender. We begin by surrendering to God. What a blessed gift surrender is! We yield our souls to the one who loves us. Early in our relationship with God, there is often a wrestling match of wills, because God's ways are not our ways. But over time, as we grow, we learn to yield. We surrender to God's love.

Abandonment. Following our surrender, we grow into a stage best described as abandonment. In this stage, while we still find a strong difference between "our way" and "God's way" in a given matter (forgiving those who have harmed us, for example), we much more readily yield to God's will. We recognize the difference between God's ways and our own, but our trust in his ways has increased. We willingly abandon ourselves to God's leading.

Contentment. Beyond abandonment, the soul grows into a stage marked by contentment. Not passivity, but contentment. We begin to experience every aspect of our lives—the good and the bad, the easy and the hard—as people who are deeply loved by a good God. In a world gone mad, we maintain a deep trust that God is moving through history to accomplish his purposes. We lay aside our self-defined agendas—even for how we think we'll achieve God-honoring goals—and receive tragedies and victories alike in faith that God is in control.

To this point, much of what Willard has described parallels the experience of a believer who is Journeying Together, learning the disciplines of the spiritual life and becoming more aware of his or her inner brokenness and dependence on God. Those who emerge from the desert experience of "hitting bottom" possess a deeply rooted contentment. This leads to the final stage discussed by Willard—the move toward participation.

Participation. Flowing out of our contentment is the potential to experience an even deeper connection with God as our souls come to a place of participation. This deep involvement is what many ancient

Christian writers referred to as *unity* or oneness with God, which Jesus prayed we would experience (John 17:21).

Like supple gloves over the hand of God, our wills become so conformed to his and our character so similar to his that we move, speak, lead, and serve as members of his body. We participate in God's activity here on earth under his direction and at his bidding, guided by his hand and marked by his character. This deeply interconnected life is what Jesus promised would bear much fruit (John 15:5).

The key to participation — and the reason I love Willard's use of that word — is that when we're in that place of deep union and oneness with God, when we're growing and increasingly seeing the world through his eyes, nothing we do is about perfection or legalistically "achieving" a certain state of super-spirituality. Instead, we are focused on the invitation of the moment, in which God is leading us day by day. We *participate with God* in the circumstances of everyday life.

Those who live this way are a force to be reckoned with! Those who are yielded, malleable, and willing to go wherever God leads and do whatever God requires are a powerful tool in his hands. They are people who have died to themselves and who say each day, "I have been crucified with Christ and I no longer live, but Christ lives in me. The life I now live in the body, I live by faith in the Son of God, who loved me and gave himself for me" (Galatians 2:20). No matter how humble the assignment, they pursue life *from a place of deep participation with God*. They are no longer striving to achieve or prove themselves. They are no longer seeking to overcome the sin that defined their past. They are not trying to achieve something *for* God. Instead, out of the depth of their relationship with God, they move as the Spirit leads.

This level of selflessness is a key marker of the Following Together stage. Whereas a hunger to learn and grow is a mark of the first stage and a growing dependence is a mark of the second, this third stage of learning to follow God together with others is marked by humility and self-sacrifice. Many of God's people long to live this way, but they've been taught to pursue it as a solo journey. Some started out well but got stuck in the desert. What they need are others who are following Jesus along with them, mature believers willing to go the distance. Even just one relationship is all that is needed sometimes to reignite the fire of their faith and get them back to running the race.

WHAT'S STIRRING?

1. Do you remember a season of life or ministry when you knew you had passed through a desert of some kind? Were you reluctant at all? Why or why not?

2. Have you been able to accept and even grow to love your own story enough to offer it to others in service to their journey? What parts of your story do you hope that God may yet redeem?

3. Which part of the progression from surrender to participation do you find yourself in right now?

4. Who are the people walking with you during this season of life?

CHAPTER 6
RUNNING TOGETHER

Two of my sons have been high school varsity cross-country runners. I'm amazed to see how—in all weather conditions, at all times of the day—they find great joy in running. It's hard for me to imagine feeling joy when I think about running. But I cannot deny what I see. All summer long and several months into the school year they exude a palpable sense of excitement.

My sons often choose to run with their friends. They enjoy the camaraderie. But as they have improved, gaining speed and developing endurance, I've noticed they tend to run with friends who match or exceed their own abilities. Why? They want to be pushed. They want to be challenged. They want to continue growing.

Mature Christ followers have been around long enough to know that relationships are one of the keys to ongoing growth. But they have also found that the kinds of relationships they need aren't always the kind the local church encourages or provides. So, for example, while a traditional small group is wonderful for someone new to the faith who is eager to learn, it is unlikely to meet the developmental needs of someone in this stage of Following Together. Most often, this person gets tapped to lead these groups, but serving as a leader tends to be more of a ministry to others, not something that directly facilitates his or her own growth. In some cases, ministry leaders consider these mature believers "renegades" if they choose not to participate in a church's small group structure. By doing this, churches may inadvertently prevent these deeply surrendered people from finding the very relationships they need to stay the course.

When mature believers are relegated to relational structures that don't meet their needs, they experience loneliness — "sole care" rather than "soul care" — right in the midst of community. And it's a painful experience. They know the value of community and have taught it to others, but now they find themselves on a solitary journey, running the race alone. Maybe that's where you are today. Perhaps it's why you picked up this book. Maybe you know firsthand what it's like to travel the path alone, and you'd love it if your church recognized an alternative for mature believers.

Those who enter the Following Together stage of growth no longer need highly structured, directionally focused relationships. What they need are mutual and collaborative relationships with other Christ followers. At this stage, the ways we help each other grow do not depend on structures and directives but on our shared posture as *followers* of God.

SIGNS OF LIFE

The relationships most needed at this stage are characterized by mutual leadership (low on direction, high on discernment) and can take on various forms. In this section, I hope to provide a few practical suggestions you can use to nurture these relationships in your own life and among those in your faith community. There are a number of signs of life you may experience in yourself or observe in others who are moving into the Following Together stage:

1. Increased willingness to admit mistakes and to be honest about areas of struggle and ongoing sin

2. Openness to seek help when needed
3. Growing commitment to engage the world through authentic service, coupled with periods of disengaging for retreat and recovery
4. Ability to accurately name strengths and weaknesses
5. Embrace of suffering as a God-graced means of growth and refinement
6. Ability to engage in sacrificial service
7. Sense of fulfillment that comes from being used by God in unique ways, whether in obscurity or in the limelight

BALANCING DIRECTION AND DISCERNMENT

Healthy relationships at this stage flourish because they are based on giving and receiving the gift of discernment. Direction, if it is needed at all, typically comes when a person is willingly participating in a structured group format or in a spiritual director relationship.

Spiritual Transformation in Relationships

| Stage 1: | Stage 2: | **STAGE 3:** |
| Learning Together | Journeying Together | **Following Together** |

Direction

Because relationships that encourage growth are more flexible and loosely structured, they are ideally suited for those who bear leadership responsibilities, whether in vocational ministry or some other context. As noted earlier, life itself is the curriculum for a growing relationship with God. God's activity in and around a person is the primary subject of discussion, prayer, and conversation.

At times, there can be some direction in the relationship, most notably through asking appropriate questions that guide the conversation. Sometimes these questions will be asked directly; sometimes they are implied indirectly. People may from time to time ask each other questions like these:

- What do you discern God is doing within you?
- What do you discern God is doing around you?
- How are you responding to God's activity?
- How can I/we help you or pray for you?

In my experience, these questions are not always explicitly asked. Instead, they are the undercurrent of the conversation. They may pop up from time to time in an explicit inquiry, but more often they are the subtext beneath what is said.

Discernment

Discernment plays a critical role in this stage of growth. In particular, a growing disciple needs help in three key areas: (1) seeing beyond their own perspective, (2) recognizing God's assignments, and (3) staying attentive to God's ongoing transformation in their life.

God's perspective. Fellow runners give voice to evidence of God's work in a person's life. They offer help in discerning the difference between invitations from God and circumstances that are really just distractions. When I need help discerning in this way, I fill people in on the circumstances and ask them to help me see what is happening from God's perspective.

God's assignments. Sometimes we feel deeply called to one area of work or ministry but then get swept up into another path. Or we're immersed in our current work, but something new is stirring that involves greater risk. As we discern together the opportunities and stirrings, we are better able to give a wholehearted yes to every next step of following, no matter how challenging or difficult that step may be.

I once shared with a friend that I had a sense God might be inviting me to consider a position with greater leadership responsibilities, but I was fearful of presuming too much. He commented that, if anything, my tendency at that time seemed more inclined to step away from such opportunities rather than move presumptively toward them. Knowing my tendencies, he discerned that what I was sensing was indeed an invitation from God to consider new opportunities.

God's ongoing transformation. At this stage, believers are aware of their story, their brokenness, and their need for God. Yet they still need folks who will help them name the subtle and not-so-subtle ways they are resisting God's ongoing work.

One of my spiritual friends knows my tendency to isolate as a form of self-protection. It's a behavior that damages the very relationships I value and need most. This isolation impairs my ability to carry out the mission God has given me. Such self-protection is one of the things that easily entangles me. I need to throw it off as sin to have any hope of running the race marked out for me. This friend loves me enough to discern when I'm falling into this trap. They are not judgmental or unkind, but they share in truth what they observe. I would be an absolute fool not to heed such words from a friend.

FINDING THE RIGHT RELATIONAL FORMAT

Relationships in the Following Together stage are just as important as they are in earlier stages, and several of them overlap with structures in the previous stages. In this stage, they don't require the same level of structure to support them; they tend to happen more naturally.

Spiritual Friendship. As senior pastor of the multisite LifeChurch. tv, Craig Groeschel leads one of the fastest-growing churches in the country. In order to keep his faith strong in the midst of unrelenting ministry demands, Craig recognized that having spiritual friends in his life was essential for his ongoing growth and maturity: "One of the elements that was missing for years was ongoing spiritual friendships. Not 'I'm Pastor Craig and you're in my small group.' But 'I'm Craig and you're a peer Christian and you have the right to speak into my life to help correct me.' Having those relationships with other believers has been a huge part of my spiritual development."[1]

I briefly discussed spiritual friendship as a relational format for those in the Journeying Together stage, and it's also an important kind of relationship for those in the Following Together stage. The difference is in the depth and focus of the relationship. Spiritual friendships can be deepened in a variety of ways, but primarily through three means:

- *Self-disclosure.* Who are you under the surface? At this point, we see a broadening of self-disclosure from the categories of our personality and family of origin to the deeper waters of ongoing sinful struggles and habits. These are forms of self-disclosure, where, increasingly, we understand the importance of having our "dark side" — our broken, negative, and sinful patterns — known by others.

- *Prayer.* Praying together is one of the most powerful ways to deepen these mutual relationships. When you pray, do it with a clear eye on where God is at work in the world around us. These prayers bring great joy to God and unleash power in the spiritual realm. Mountains get moved, chains of bondage are broken, and destinies unfold. The work of prayer changes the world.

- *Serving Together.* As God leads you, begin to share responsibly in efforts to improve the world and to reach out to those in need with the love of Christ. Great things can be accomplished through strong friendships centered on a common love for God. Can you imagine the energy that would be unleashed for the kingdom of God if more and more mature believers were to become friends?

Spiritual Direction. Just as with spiritual friendships, it is common for spiritual direction to continue into the Following Together stage, with some deepening of the relationship from the previous stage. As we mature, our need for direction decreases as a greater emphasis is placed on exercising discernment.

Perhaps the best way to illustrate this is to introduce you to my spiritual director, Linda Richardson. Several years ago, when my day-to-day responsibilities shifted and disrupted several of my close relationships, I sought spiritual direction. I knew I needed someone to walk with me in a discerning way, and a friend gave me Linda's name.

Linda was spiritually attentive to this season of my journey with God, and her wise counsel and prayer led me to a newfound dependency on God. I began to rely on the Lord in very practical ways each day, and I became more aware of additional brokenness in my heart. Linda helped me see these things and taught me to pay attention to my heart. That's what a good spiritual director does.

I asked Linda to describe the work she does with her directees and to share why people typically search for a spiritual director in the first place:

Why would people who are solidly evangelical, who have been reading and studying their Bibles somewhat regularly and have a prayer life, want or need to see a spiritual director? When I asked myself that question almost twenty years ago, it dawned on me, as a church leader, that it was rare that anyone ever asked me about my spiritual life. It was assumed I was doing well.

But we aren't always doing well. Our spiritual lives cycle in and out of warmth and coldness, dryness and vitality, and that movement is often related to what's going on in our lives. We can be thrown off by life changes, by hitting a wall spiritually because of a crisis, by disappointment with God, or by sin in our lives that is resistant to change. We may be in a time of discernment and decision, be spiritually restless, or realize the spiritual disciplines that have been nurturing us are no longer helpful. On the positive side, sometimes God may be leading us into a new place spiritually or theologically or into a new understanding of his nature. We may be longing for integration of head and heart or be experiencing a deepening hunger for God.

For these and other reasons, mature Christians seek out spiritual direction, a relationship of spiritual companionship or friendship. In a spiritual direction relationship, the directee is given an opportunity to tell their story in an unhurried way to someone who listens thoughtfully and seeks to discern the movement of God in the individual's life. The spiritual director's role is to notice where the Holy Spirit is already working and to encourage the directee to listen to their own heart and to what

God may be saying about the next step on their spiritual journey.

The directee is free to bring whatever they want to talk about to a monthly session. Because we are holistic beings, any subject is appropriate to share, though the focus of spiritual direction is always on the directee's relationship with God.

At the beginning of a spiritual direction session, the directee and I will often observe a few minutes of silence to allow the distractions and rushed feelings to subside and the heart concerns to surface in the directee. We may do a directed silent meditation to facilitate letting go and receiving. Silence may also be appropriate later in a session when we are listening for the Lord's direction together.

Questions are at the core of most spiritual direction. I often ask, "How is your soul?" which may prompt the directee to go back into silence to discern an answer. In the beginnings of a spiritual direction relationship, it is often important to have the directee ponder questions like "How do you connect with God?" "When do you feel closest to God?" or "What do you think God might be saying?"

When meeting with a directee, observing their body posture can be very important. Are they sitting on the edge of their chair, are their arms folded, are they making eye contact, are there tears, do they seem anxious or relaxed? Being aware of body postures often helps me know how best to communicate to the directee that they are in a safe place.

In the silence or while listening to the directee, sometimes a Scripture will come to my mind or the directee's mind. If the text stays with me, I may ask the directee to close their eyes while I read it aloud slowly two or three times. I may suggest they write the verse(s) on a card and carry it with them, or I may suggest they read the Scripture each day for a month.

Prayer in a variety of forms is frequently included in a spiritual direction session. We may use a Scripture to pray from, such as "The Spirit God gave us does not make us timid" (2 Timothy 1:7).

I might suggest we prayerfully breathe in the words "be still" and breathe out "and know that I am God" (Psalm 46:10). Liturgical prayer can provide words for prayer when the directee has no words of their own. Sometimes spontaneous or healing prayer can be powerful. I frequently anoint with oil and pray a blessing over a directee or pray with the laying on of hands, addressing their soul needs as we end our time together. Confession may be appropriate at times—always in the context of trust and confidentiality.

If a pattern of concerns begins to emerge that might require psychological counseling or marital therapy, a spiritual director may urge the directee to pursue that kind of help instead of or in addition to spiritual direction.

The spiritual director is a witness to another's life through the exciting as well as the mundane moments. Because the spiritual direction relationship is not crisis oriented, the relationship may go on for years. The continuous monthly meetings communicate to the directee that their story is worth telling and worth hearing but do not foster an unhealthy dependency on the spiritual director. In the ancient practice of spiritual direction, the directee is companioned and loved on the journey toward a deepening intimacy with God. That, in itself, can bring rest to our anxious, overly busy, striving souls.

As Linda makes clear, people seek out a spiritual director for a variety of reasons. For some, it is a season of hunger for a deeper walk with God. For others, there is a life change, a crisis situation, or a major decision that requires discernment and wisdom. Still others simply long for mature spiritual friendship, for a companion who will walk with them as they follow Christ together. Church leaders, in particular, are quite vulnerable to isolation and often find ordinary relationships challenging, given their leadership visibility. For pastors and those in public positions of leadership, a spiritual director can be a fabulous way to find a safe place, a place of rest for their souls. Linda mentioned that she often shares Jeremiah 6:16

with those looking for a spiritual director—the verse where Jeremiah speaks of those who are asking for the ancient path, the good way of life that gives rest to the soul: "Stand at the crossroads and look; ask for the ancient paths, ask where the good way is, and walk in it, and you will find rest for your souls." This is what a spiritual director can provide—a relationship of rest for a weary soul.

Group Spiritual Direction. Group spiritual direction draws on the same aspirations of individual spiritual direction but opens the experience to input from a group of people. Spiritual director Alice Fryling describes it this way in *Seeking God Together*:

> The format is simple. The group starts with a time of silence or a short meditation. After that the group invites one person to talk for five or ten minutes about whatever they'd like. Then there is another time of prayerful silence. Out of the silence, the group begins to ask questions, responding to whatever the directee is presenting. At the close of the person's presentation and the group's response, there is another time of prayerful silence during which each person in the group prays silently for the individual who presented. The group may choose to allow time for two people to present in one session, but in any case, over the course of several months, everyone will have the opportunity to be the directee.
>
> The purpose of these groups is not counseling or therapy. Nor are they intended to be places where we can engage in aimless, self-absorbed conversations. The purpose of spiritual direction groups is *formation*. Spiritual formation is "a process of being conformed to the image of Christ for the sake of others." The intentional goal of group spiritual direction is to help each participant become more aware of God in their lives, *for the sake of others*. In other words, it leads to an awakening of the soul. This awakening then leads to a life that is purposeful and intentional. Group spiritual direction helps individuals grow in their faith, love others more fully, and participate in the mission of the church more effectively.[2]

Several different formats and a number of helpful resources exist for those interested in finding out more about group spiritual direction. A formal group spiritual direction process can be highly instructive for mature believers who are learning to follow Christ together.

FINDING THE RIGHT ... FOLLOWERS

The best leaders for individuals in this stage are their peers, other believers who are also in this stage — people who attend to God's activity within, pursue new areas of personal growth and development, and obediently follow whatever hard assignments they receive from God. The table below will be helpful as you identify these people in your congregation:

Leadership Qualities	Spiritual Gifts
• Knowledge of their own dark side and ability to listen to others talk about their dark side • Ability to discern Jesus' voice and to obey • Strong faith in God's loving presence and rule over all • Willingness to follow through on hard assignments • Increased level of prayerfulness and sensitivity to spiritual warfare, and an ability to persevere despite suffering and opposition	• Shepherding • Encouragement • Leadership • Discernment • Mercy

These folks are well versed in their own story, and they are able to articulate their areas of brokenness, weakness, and failure. They know where they have failed and understand the power of sin and how to confront it with grace and truth. There is no pretense, no posturing, no image management. They regularly demonstrate a sustained and selfless interest in the needs of others. Most of them have a capacity for deep listening, marked by high levels of empathy. They are able to enter into someone else's experience, but without making the focus of the conversation about them.

Fellow followers seek to truly *discern Jesus' voice* — in their own lives and as they listen to someone else. Spiritual directors often describe their own ministry in these terms. They see their task as one of listening to God in behalf of their directee and bringing into the conversation what they sense God is saying. As a result, they can speak things into a directee's life that come straight from the heart of God.

Five Questions for Those Who Are Following Together

1. What has God been stirring in you recently? What are you learning? Where have you sensed resistance to God? Where have you sensed a feeling of anointing over your work?
2. What spiritual practices have been keeping your soul in a connected place these days?
3. Are you getting enough time for silence and solitude — times when you don't need to be productive? How can I help you in that?
4. What are you afraid of as you consider new areas of obedience?
5. How can I pray for you — not for your work, your relatives, or your family, though all those things are important — but specifically how can I pray for *you*?

I recall a time when I was with my friend Troy at Starbucks, and as I listened to him, I felt God nudging me. I sensed Troy's interior world was in a unique kind of conflict — and the phrase "blessed mutiny" came to my mind. I wasn't trying to figure out a clever way to describe his journey; I was just listening — to God and to him. And those were the words that came to mind quite clearly — a "blessed mutiny." I chose to share this phrase with Troy, and it became an image he held on to. It helped him realize that God could bring something good out of the chaos and confusion of this season in his life.

Those in the Following Together stage also exude what Quaker author Thomas Kelly calls "cosmic patience." In *A Testament of Devotion,* Kelly writes of those who feel a sense of urgency for the cause of God and want to fulfill assignments when God asks. They do not fret or wring their hands in fear of what may come. Rather, as Kelly writes, "It is a life that is freed from strain and anxiety and hurry, for something of the Cosmic Patience of God becomes ours. Are our lives *unshakable,* because we are clear down on bed rock, rooted and grounded in the love of God? This is the first and the great commandment."[3]

A mentor named Phyllis Anne exuded this strong confidence, a quality of being unshakable. She taught me many things as my mentor, particularly because my husband and I had only been married for a few years. So my conversations with Phyllis Anne naturally turned toward how my marriage was integrating with my personal walk with God. As we continued to meet over many weeks and months, a vivid image came to mind. I pictured myself as a tiny little Jet Ski and Phyllis Anne as a massive aircraft carrier. While I was busy buzzing over the waves, making lots of noise and activity, winding about in random directions, she was stable, strong, and sure of her path. I saw a calm patience, a person following a steady course that was rooted in her deep trust in God. In her presence, I found myself slowing down, and when I left our times together, I felt steady and assured. Ironically, during the time she served as my mentor, she was experiencing a great deal of turbulence in her life. In the midst of all the change and chaos around her, she stood strong, fully herself, able to give to others.

One final quality I find in those who are committed to the long haul, seeking to persevere in following God, is a high level of prayerfulness — one that is not weird, forced, or mechanical. They recognize that God is the invisible participant in all of life — present in every conversation, every challenge, every opportunity, every open door, and every closed door. They know that God sees every tear, every hope, and every fear. So it seems natural to pray to God, because prayer is simply the language of their relationship with God — and that relationship permeates everything.

Recently, a dear friend stopped by our house. She's in a season marked by growth, and we talked about what God might be inviting us to do together. Over the years, our relationship has grown through regular prayer for and with each other. Sometimes we pray in person, but just as often, we pray for each other when we are apart, as God brings the other person to mind. Sometimes she will send me a brief text or e-mail: "You're on my radar again, Mindy." Amazingly, her notes tend to arrive just as something big is brewing in my life—a new assignment, a new challenge, a new area of growth or ministry.

Those in this stage best serve one another through a variety of forms—encouragement, shepherding, challenge, mercy, and discernment. All of these are important ways we fulfill the assignments God has for us. What matters most is not the particular gifts themselves, but the fact that these relationships are marked by humility, a shared curiosity about God and God's activity around them, and a God's-eye perspective on life, particularly in the midst of suffering and struggle.

A VISION FOR THE ENTIRE JOURNEY

Church leaders and pastors can help their congregations by valuing those who are in this stage of growth, helping them remain vitally connected to the work of the church. This is important for their ongoing spiritual health and maturity. More often than not, the "vision" for community in a church focuses primarily on the early stages of spiritual growth, and as important as this is, it tends to give the impression that relationships don't matter as much beyond those early stages. Typically, spiritual growth is seen as a period of learning in community, followed by an individualistic pursuit of growth. Sometimes the church itself is seen as optional in this process.

To change this paradigm for spiritual formation in the church, pastors and leaders need to envision the kinds of relationships that mature Christians need and want. Whether by means of sermons or personal meetings with mature believers, it is important that leaders communicate a plan to help mature believers continue to grow, a plan that validates and challenges them. It is often helpful to clarify that the goal at this stage is to help them *stay the course*.

Since many of the relationships at this stage of growth are less structured and programmed, you may find that relatively little needs to be done by a church staff to create ministry "on-ramps" for these relationships. Often, folks in this stage can figure out many of the next steps on their own. A leader's primary job is to help them understand *why* it's important to be in relationship and to challenge them to continue growing and not stall.

Don't forget: one size *does not* fit all. Instead, affirm and envision those in the Following Together stage for what they are — the vibrant core of your church!

Gateway Church in Austin, Texas, does an excellent job of creating vision for relationships, particularly in this third stage of growth. Senior pastor John Burke believes deeply in the power of relationships to support authentic spiritual growth for mature believers. To communicate this he uses the metaphor of running. In fact, Gateway refers to its vision for the Following Together stage of growth as "Running Partners," and I've heard their senior staff and spiritual formation staff speak passionately about these relationships and how they are stimulating transformation in their congregation. Here is how they describe their vision for spiritual growth:

> In the same way athletes train to reach physical goals, we need spiritual training partners to provide encouragement, pacing, and motivation for spiritual goals. Running Partners encourage one another to become all God intends each person to be.
>
> *What does a Running Partner group look like?* Running Partners are most often a group of two, three, or four people. Interestingly, we've found that the most successful partners have been groups of three. This size is still small enough to make scheduling easy, but it is large enough to give good feedback and support. Running Partners are typically of the same gender, though sometimes one or two couples may form a group.
>
> *How do I choose my Running Partners?* This will sound dumb, but the best way to find a good Running Partner is simply to ask someone to be your Running Partner. Ask a friend, people in your small group, or people you serve with at church. In other words, your best option is just try it out for a while with someone who shares some of your spiritual goals.
>
> *What will happen when Running Partners meet?* The primary goal is that you will encourage one another to grow in your relationship with God. You can meet any time and place that is convenient for you and your Running Partners. It should just be a time and place that is suitable for personal, and oftentimes private, conversation.[4]

While Gateway uses the Running Partners vision for every

stage of spiritual growth, it is particularly helpful for those who are mature because it seeks to connect people through natural relationships. It provides a flexible structure that begins with some simple coaching, and then relationships tend to move to the depth level of those involved. What's important to note is that Pastor John Burke is *intentional* as he casts the vision. He isn't just offering another program or advertising a class for learning the spiritual disciplines. This isn't a small group program or a Bible study. Instead, the church places the onus of responsibility for forging and deepening relationships on the shoulders of those involved. They don't need (nor would it be healthy) to give too much structure to this. Instead, they need to cast a vision that winsomely attracts mature believers to relationships that meet them right where they are.

The Blessed Community

Thomas Kelly paints a beautiful picture of community in his essay "The Blessed Community" in *A Testament of Love*:

> In wonder and awe we find ourselves already interknit within unofficial groups of kindred souls. A "chance" conversation comes, and in a few moments we know that we have found and have been found by another member of the Blessed Community. Sometimes we are thus suddenly knit together in the bonds of a love far faster than those of many years' acquaintance. In unbounded eagerness we seek for more such fellowship, and wonder at the apparent lethargy of mere "members."
>
> In the Fellowship cultural and educational and national and racial differences are leveled. Unlettered men are at ease with the truly humble scholar who lives in the Life, and the scholar listens with joy and openness to the precious experiences of God's dealing with the workingman...
>
> The final grounds of holy Fellowship are in God. Lives immersed and drowned in God are drowned in love, and know one another in him, and know one another in love.[5]

COMMUNITY IS NOT PERFECT

Before I conclude my reflections on this stage of spiritual growth and maturity, I'd be remiss if I didn't state the obvious. Many relationships start with the promise of great impact and influence but end up causing much harm instead. Challenges exist all along the way. Betrayals, misunderstandings, selfishness, and other dead-end streets can entangle and even damage those who run this race.

I've had close relationships that ended abruptly with no opportunity for understanding how or why things went wrong. Perhaps you have had close relationships that were used for someone's personal advantage. Clearly, we should never think we've arrived—that as followers of Christ we are immune to causing or receiving this kind of pain, no matter how mature we may be. We live in a broken world, and even after we have experienced God's healing, we remain at best wounded healers—people prone to wander from the way of life. As Cornelius Plantinga writes, "Things in human life are not as they ought to be."[6] The world we live in—even within the church—is not a picture of shalom, of peace or human flourishing. Our world and our relationships continue to be marred by sin, selfish ambition, instant gratification, and downright meanness.

I once heard a best man give this toast at a wedding reception: "May you be happy together for ... [awkward silence] ... as long as you choose to be." In other words, *As long as this relationship stays comfortable and meets your personal needs better than other readily available alternatives, I hope you enjoy it. I hope you're happy as long as you're happy.* As a toast, it was a far cry from the vows the couple had just taken—to remain together for better or for worse, for richer, for poorer, in sickness and in health, till death do us part. But it accurately reflected the sad truth about how fallen human beings today understand relationships—as temporary, comfortable, convenient. To be sure, the best man was probably a bit tipsy and his words were unguarded. But in the moment, no one knew how to respond to what he had said. It was awkward but, sadly, all too true in our world today.

Relationships can be difficult. We are wounded, and so we withdraw. We are hesitant to risk opening up, so we become guarded and cautious. Unfortunately, this means our local churches are all too often communities of people who merely share a few theological concepts and enjoy a "good service" on Sunday mornings. Without the deeper relationships necessary for spiritual growth and formation, most people aren't growing as disciples. They are not experiencing the transforming, self-denying, world-impacting life with God they were promised.

So the question we face in our churches is a question of growth — a growth that requires long-term commitment. To put it simply, will we remain "fans" of Jesus, content to keep our distance and go along with the crowd? Or will we become his disciples, willing to leave everything behind to learn, to journey, and to follow our Lord and Teacher? Disciples are hungry to learn, eager to be taught. Disciples stay the course. Disciples finish the race.

Life as followers of Christ in the West will likely become harder in the days to come. Will those in our churches be prepared to face opposition, even persecution? Will we as leaders be ready to count the cost? Are you ready to run the race marked out for you?

To put it positively, are you ready for revival? What would happen if every local church *doubled in size* with brand-new Christians within the next twelve months? What would you do with these new believers? How would they grow? Who would you turn to in your church to mentor, direct, and shape their spiritual growth? Organized church activities like Sunday services and small groups will take them only so far. How will you help those who face interior brokenness grow through their pain? Will they, like others before them, have to look outside the church to find the help they need?

An interconnected community is an unstoppable force, reckless in love and vigilant in its pursuit of God. The world has seen, and could see again, the impact of such a community — surrendered, alive, and engaged.

If you aren't sure how the framework I've suggested in this book can apply to your ministry context, hang with me for a few more pages. We'll hear from a senior pastor whose church has been exceptionally effective in supporting all stages of spiritual growth, even without any specific path or operational structure in place.

Take heart! God is committed to the growth of his people. As leaders, we can learn to support God's activity of growing disciples at all stages of development by shifting our focus from programs to relationships, recognizing the unique ways God works through others to shape and mold us to become more like Jesus Christ.

WHAT'S STIRRING?

1. What differences have you observed between those who run this stage of the race alone and those who run together?

2. Is there someone running relatively alone right now who might benefit from your friendship and support? What would taking a next step toward that person mean for you?

3. What formats for discernment have been most helpful to you in the past? Structured? Unstructured? What format might be helpful to you in this next season of your life or leadership?

CONCLUSION
GIVE A FLYING RIP

A number of years ago, I began my new role on staff at Willow Creek Community Church, and I found myself sitting across the table from teaching pastor John Ortberg during a brainstorming meeting. We had been talking about the process of transformation and how small group leaders could lead in such a way that transformation would actually happen in their groups.

I asked John, "How can we help our small group leaders lead well so that transformation into Christlikeness is actually happening in the group?" John paused to ponder the question and then began to name several essential qualities for a leader to develop. He mentioned the importance of possessing listening skills, discernment to offer spiritual guidance, empathy, wisdom, and a heart for prayer.

I dutifully took notes and began imagining how I might work with our small group ministry to develop those skills in our leaders. To be honest, I felt a bit overwhelmed. I thought of the small group leaders I've known through the years. Were they really thinking about all of this when they led? Did they have the time and desire to invest in learning and developing all of these skills? Could I even do all of this?

I set down my pen and looked up. In all seriousness, I asked, "Don't you think small group leaders really just need to *give a flying rip* about someone else's spiritual development?" I'm not sure what that phrase actually means, but somehow it seemed fitting.

Throwing back his head, laughing, he said, "If you can figure out how to get people to do *that*, none of the rest of this matters."

Now, of course, the other things John mentioned really do matter. They are wonderful skills that help people grow and are key tools in the process of spiritual formation. But skills and tools won't matter if there isn't a fundamental *caring*—a passionate desire to see God at work in just one person. When one person takes an authentic interest in someone else, qualities like discernment, direction, and prayer move from being mechanical steps for successful leadership to behaviors that naturally characterize our relationships. The "flying rip" is really another way of saying that our leadership of and service to others are rooted in genuine love for them. Even if we do it imperfectly (and we will), when we authentically care, it can cover over a multitude of relational missteps.

PALM VALLEY CHURCH: A CHURCH THAT GIVES A FLYING RIP

I first encountered the ministry of Palm Valley Church in 2010 when I met their teaching pastor, Jerrell Jobe. I was invited to be a guest speaker for his master's degree program in spiritual formation and leadership, and he explained that Palm Valley, a church of several thousand members in south Texas, was deeply committed to spiritual formation and the process of discipleship. That caught my attention! I was eager to learn more.

On weekends, Palm Valley Church looks like any other large church. But beyond the weekend services and midweek "New Community" services, there are only a few organized small groups scattered here and there, and relatively few programs. There isn't a women's ministry or a men's ministry. It's a simple church. But there is another story beneath the surface—a "story behind the story."

Several years ago, Rick Gannon, who is now the senior pastor at Palm Valley, led a local expression of a three-year discipleship program called Master's Commission. Participants in the program relocated to Palm Valley to join this rigorous, life-on-life, immersion experience. Every year, around thirty students joined the program, living in dormitories, studying together, and learning to live out in a practical way what it means to be a disciple of Jesus. The program wasn't an official ministry of the church, but the participants served within Palm Valley Church as part of their experience.

The first year of the program began by teaching students to develop a humble posture before the Lord. It didn't matter who you were or how impressive your résumé was, you had to, in Rick's words, "drop your baggage at the door." As the first-year students spent time learning together, this quickly morphed into deep journeying together. Many of the students experienced times of brokenness followed by healing. In the second year, students took on apprenticeship roles and shadowed senior church leaders in hands-on ministry. Some ended the program at that point, but those who chose to continue to the third and final year took on more responsibility for a specific area of ministry.

When the senior pastor of Palm Valley Church retired in 2002, he asked Rick to take over leadership of the church. Though other staff members had more theological education, the pastor knew Rick had a strong passion for the Great Commission and was living in simple trust in and obedience to God. He was making disciples who were leading fruitful lives for the kingdom.

Rick was shocked at the invitation. Though he and his wife, Teri, had served as missionaries in Moscow, they had no ambitions for leading a local church. But after much prayer and soul-searching before the Lord, Rick and Teri accepted the leadership role. Over the next ten years, Palm Valley Church experienced explosive growth, adding services, buildings, and staff. Like many other churches with a dynamic communicator, they grew and thrived.

Whenever the church had a new staff position to fill, can you guess where Rick looked to fill the position? He always looked back to those he had discipled through Master's Commission or checked in with people who led similar ministries and asked for referrals. Why? There was a shared history and trust, as well as a shared commitment to making disciples. In some cases, Rick had worked side by side with a person for years in a context outside the church, so it made sense to bring in those he knew and trusted.

While the thriving ministry at Palm Valley looks similar to other large churches, there is a key difference: virtually the entire staff—*and* their spouses—have been trained through the same process of discipleship. In many cases, the staff and spouses have been *personally* nurtured and developed by Rick and Teri. Through my work at Willow Creek, I've come to know leaders at many large churches around the country, and I can't think of a single one who had this level of shared relational and spiritual equity. Most adult Christians I meet have never had *any* formal discipleship process, and those who have are typically no longer relationally connected to those who once poured into their lives.

What is the point of sharing this story? I share it because underneath the surface, Palm Valley isn't like most other churches at all. That's not just my opinion; it's supported by research. You see, when Palm Valley Church took the REVEAL Spiritual Life Survey several years ago, they had one of the highest spiritual vitality scores of any church that had taken the survey.[1] Palm Valley's "results," like those of other spiritually vital churches, stem from the clear vision for discipleship and formation among those who lead the church. This is a church laser-focused on being disciples and building disciples. Everything they do serves those purposes.

These leaders—and the people in this church—*give a flying rip.*

Currently, the leadership of Palm Valley is exploring how to provide a more accessible and intentional spiritual growth path for their members. They're always pushing for more, not willing to settle for the status quo. They aren't interested in simply increasing growth in attendance, having a bigger budget, or hiring more staff. They want more of God, and they have a desire to see transformation among the people they reach out to and serve.

I am confident that God will provide what they need, and more. The key to healthy spiritual transformation in a local church is ultimately not found in a particular system or programmatic structure. These can be helpful tools, but ultimately transformation is the result of the Spirit of God at work in the lives of people through relationships within the body of Christ. Transformation is the fruit of the Spirit as followers of Christ love one another, speak truth to one another, listen to one another, care for one another, and bear one another's burdens. In all of this, dependence on God is the key. I don't want to sound simplistic. I love thinking of and planning systems and structures. But transformation in the local church really is as simple as caring for other people. Caring for their souls, for their hearts. Anyone, anywhere, in Jesus' name, can do that—including you.

A focus on making disciples isn't theoretical; it's something we do as part of everyday life. "Discipleship is not like building a building," Rick explains. "It's more like making sausages. It's ugly and messy and sometimes feels like three steps backward. But everyone has a next step. Those words give hope to everyone. My life might be a total shipwreck, or I might be busy raising kids and paying a mortgage, but there is a next step for every 'me' around here as we are transformed into the image of Jesus."

Since Rick has experienced God's blessing in raising up disciples in his local church, I've asked him to share some of the "nonnegotiables" he and his team live with at Palm Valley. In sharing these, the goal is not to copy or reproduce what they have done, but to find inspiration and fresh ideas for your own ministry context.

Spiritual Formation Nonnegotiables

1. The pastor must take the lead. Life produces life. You cannot give what you do not have. You don't delegate the formation of souls to another; it's a burden of all the staff—chiefly the senior leadership.
2. Discipleship must never be limited to just a decision, but rather it requires a lifetime of practice. We are con-

stantly thinking of ways to get people focused on the journey as the destination.

3. Scripture must be *applied* to people's lives. The Word is power. We try to always teach for change. Give the people something to do or to be in response to truth.

4. We must remember that the process of discipleship is unlike most of what pastors do in today's church world. It's not clean — like a building project that has a start and completion date. Spiritual growth is never so easily defined.

5. Transformation of souls must affect every area of the church. It's not just a class or a department. It's not just for new believers or those who seem to be really struggling with sin. It's for everyone. In light of that, leaders must have a deep conviction that everyone's formation is still in process.

6. Spiritual practices must regularly be taught, explained, shared in testimonies, and held up as habits of healthy, vibrant believers. We work to incorporate a wide variety of practices within our services.

7. We must set the expectation right away with new attendees. The goal of the church is disciple making. And so we have to change the scoreboard for success.

8. As the church grows larger, we must constantly look for smaller, deeper relationship settings. Many times, these settings will appear simple, organic ... and disorganized.

WHAT IS YOUR NEXT STEP?

I hope you've begun to dream a bit about the future. What can you do to see increased relational connections and transformation in your own context? In a way similar to what happened with Rick and his team, I hope you will begin with a season of prayer and discernment rather than jumping in headfirst to change your systems and structures. A word of caution before you begin: focus on changing the areas where God has given you direct influence as opposed to the things over which you have legitimate concern but no direct influence. This will help you be constructive rather than critical of others. It can also be helpful to write down your ideas, distinguishing what is truly within your "circle of influence" from that which is in your "circle of concern." As author Stephen Covey suggests, proactive people will gravitate toward the things that are within their control, the things they can directly influence. In contrast, reactive people will tend to unwisely waste energy on things over which they have no control.[2]

I saw this tension play out several years ago when I led a prayer team ministry at my church. Faithful volunteers with a passion for prayer recruited and trained intercessors, and they worked tirelessly to increase the practice of prayer within our congregation. They were highly committed to what they were called by God to do, and they operated within their circle of influence. Unfortunately, they also sought to take ownership over an area in which they didn't have influence or responsibility. They mapped out an entire teaching series focused on prayer for the midweek service. While this was a great idea, they had no influence over the planning for that service. Then they became agitated and indignant when the teaching series failed to materialize. Though their concerns were good and valid, they should not have owned them in the way they did.

I loved these volunteers, and they deeply loved God. But their desire for a greater experience of prayer at our church became consumed by things over which they had no control, taking time away from the things they could do. I share this story because all of us find ourselves here from time to time. We want changes that aren't ours to make. It's easy to be seduced by the time-wasting practice of dreaming about things that could be and maybe should be, but over which we have no control or influence. We become critical, not constructive. Even worse, we waste time and energy that could have been directed to tasks that God *has* called us to do. *Lord, have mercy.*

It may be that God has given you "eyes to see" what is needed, even over an area that is not under your direct influence or control. Receive that as an invitation from the Lord to pray. God is inviting you to be a significant part of bringing forth something new, and it will begin with your prayers. Others may eventually carry the torch or take more active and public roles in leading the way. But that is not what matters. Start by praying for what can be.

As you think about the process of spiritual formation and discipleship in your church, stop and take a moment to do this exercise.

What would you put in your circle of influence? Write those things in the outer circle.

As you look over this list, try to prioritize the steps you can take right now. What is a possible next action step in this area?

Think about the things that fit into your circle of concern. Write these down as well. This is now your prayer list.

Focus your energy and efforts on the things you can do from the first list, and faithfully bring to God in prayer whatever resides on the second. Whether you are involved directly (in leadership) or indirectly (through prayer), you play a significant role in bringing about the good things that God is working in your church to accomplish.

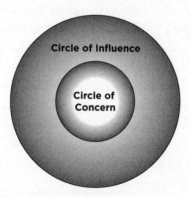

"IN ALL THINGS GOD WORKS ..."

One of the most beloved and oft-quoted verses for encouragement and hope in troubled times is Romans 8:28. You likely know it: "And we know that in all things God works for the good of those who love him, who have been called according to his purpose." I find it encouraging to know that the sovereign God works to orchestrate all of life for our ultimate good. This is a wonderful and amazing truth! But in subtle ways, this verse can be hijacked by our consumeristic, narcissistic understanding of life with God. It can be turned from an assurance of God's loving care in the midst of pain and difficulties into a promise that God will make everything *feel good* for us at all times, that he is promising to make us comfortable, satisfied, and prosperous. Some take this verse to mean that our comfort is the supreme objective, the highest good in God's purposes on earth. This misunderstanding is the complete opposite of what the verse means, and it doesn't match the call to carry our cross and endure suffering and persecution for the sake of Christ.

Several years ago, I noticed a small raised letter after the word *who* in that verse. The text note in the NIV alerted readers to another possible rendering of the original Greek text: "And we know that in all things God works together with those who love him to bring about what is good."

You may want to read that again.

This alternate rendering brings a nuance that eliminates the option of defining our "good" to fit our own desires. Instead, we hear with fresh clarity the real message of this passage—that at all times, in all things, we can have confidence that God is working to bring about what is good. God works with us to do this good. Romans 8:28 is not a passive reassurance of God's care; it's a call to action—to engagement and participation in the work that God is doing.

What kinds of people are most likely to be used by God, to work with God, in bringing about this good? Who is best able to notice and respond to the activity of God? Who is poised to respond to the world's needs in a way of deep goodness? It's people who are on the journey of transformation. They have been prepared and equipped for the selfless sacrifice needed to bring God's goodness into everyday circumstances.

How might God want to work with you to bring about what is good? And how might he work through an entire community to bring about what is good? Jesus has been clear that this redemption, this restoration, is the purpose of his earthly ministry, which continues now through his body — the church.

BRINGING WHAT IS GOOD

Through the prophet Isaiah, God foretold to his people the work his Messiah would accomplish under his power:

> The Spirit of the Sovereign LORD is on me,
>> because the LORD has anointed me
>> to proclaim good news to the poor.
> He has sent me to bind up the brokenhearted,
>> to proclaim freedom for the captives
>> and release from darkness for the prisoners,
> to proclaim the year of the LORD's favor
>> and the day of vengeance of our God,
> to comfort all who mourn,
>> and provide for those who grieve in Zion —
> to bestow on them a crown of beauty
>> instead of ashes,
> the oil of joy
>> instead of mourning,
> and a garment of praise
>> instead of a spirit of despair.
>
> — Isaiah 61:1–3

God tells us about the work of one who would function in God's intended ways — a Messiah who will unleash a wave of human flourishing. This is God's goodness being done on earth as in heaven. God's Messiah will bring shalom — peace and harmony among God's people.

The poor receive good news; the brokenhearted are bound up; the captives and prisoners are released — and the list goes on. It is a profound reversal of "the way things are" to "the way God intends for them to be." All heads turn in awe toward God in the aftermath of such heaven-instigated restoration of human flourishing. Those who

> "The webbing together of God, humans, and all creation in justice, fulfillment, and delight is what the Hebrew prophets call *shalom*. We call it peace, but it means far more than mere peace of mind or a cease-fire between enemies. In the Bible, shalom means *universal flourishing, wholeness, and delight* — a rich state of affairs in which natural needs are satisfied and natural gifts fruitfully employed, a state of affairs that inspires joyful wonder as its Creator and Savior opens doors and welcomes the creatures in whom he delights. Shalom, in other words, is the way things ought to be."
>
> **Cornelius Plantinga, *Not the Way It's Supposed to Be***

flourish become as a grove of mature, lovely oaks — effortlessly displaying the splendor of God.

Jesus, in announcing himself as Israel's Messiah, begins his public ministry by reading this passage from Isaiah (Luke 4:18 – 19). What Isaiah foretold centuries earlier is now to be fulfilled in the ministry of Jesus. And in the pages of Luke's gospel, we see Jesus bringing good news to the poor, proclaiming freedom to those in prison, bringing recovery of sight, and setting the oppressed free — opening wide the doorway to God's favor.

As we think about our own context today, how does this messianic work continue among us as the people of God? In what way is Jesus *still* bringing good news to the poor, proclaiming freedom to the captives, providing the recovery of sight for the blind, setting the oppressed free, and releasing people into God's favor? Has Jesus stopped doing these things since he is no longer physically among us?

Of course not. These manifestations of the kingdom are every bit as present today. But we understand that they happen through the ministry of the church — the people of God. The church is the *ecclesia*, the "called-out ones," and the people of God are still carrying out the messianic assignment given to them by Jesus. Before returning to heaven, Jesus said to his followers, "As the Father has sent me, I am sending you" (John 20:21). "Whoever believes in me will do the works I have been doing, and they will do even greater things than these, because I am going to the Father" (John 14:12). "All authority in heaven and on earth has been given to me. Therefore go and make disciples ..." (Matthew 28:18–19). Today, we go into the world in the name of Jesus—on the authority and in the power that he has given to us—to continue the outworking of kingdom power being exercised on earth as it is in heaven (Matthew 6:10).

PERSONAL MESSES MADE CLEAN

The gospel of John records the socially awkward beginning of Jesus' final dinner with his closest followers on the night of his betrayal. Though none of the disciples were willing to wash the feet of their fellow followers, Jesus takes the initiative and washes their feet, modeling the path of servanthood that his followers struggled to embrace. When Jesus begins to wash the feet of Peter, Peter recoils and pulls away. He does not want Jesus to do this for him, and he refuses to allow it. Peter can't accept the humiliating service of his Master in washing his dirty feet. When Jesus insists, Peter characteristically tries to turn all of this into something more significant, something that would set this uncharacteristic foot washing apart as special and important. Again, Jesus refuses. He says he is here to clean feet, nothing more, nothing less. This strikes at the heart of the matter—at Peter's pride.

Lately I've been learning a bit more about the significance of this act of cleaning. You may recall that under Jewish law, being ritually clean or unclean was extraordinarily important. Most of the Jewish dietary and behavioral code centered on remaining ceremonially "clean," and there was a long list of intentional or unintentional events that could render a person unclean. The flow of energy was always from unclean to clean. If an unclean person or animal (or even a dish) touched something clean, the clean became unclean. It was always this way, never the other way around.

Then, with the ministry of Jesus, everything changes. When Jesus touches unclean, leprous skin, it becomes clean with his touch. The unclean bleeding woman becomes clean with a touch from his garment. The unclean spirits leave a troubled soul at the touch of Jesus. Jesus passes this ability to turn the unclean clean to his followers as well. Through the power of the Holy Spirit, the unclean is made clean again. The ministry of Jesus is a ministry of cleaning — of restoring what has been dirtied and broken.

UNLESS I WASH YOU

Reading through the story of the washing of Peter's feet, I find myself drawn into the scene. Like Peter, I find myself recoiling at the thought of my Lord stooping to clean my dirty, gross, ugly, tired feet. Ick. I rarely touch my own feet.

But I also sense God asking me a question: "Mindy, don't you see that my people have been doing this for you lately? They have touched the dirty, gross, ugly, tired, and painful parts of your life, and through their touch I am making you clean again. I am healing you. I am setting you free." The awareness that Jesus is personally ministering to us through our relationships in the body of Christ needs to hit us in the gut. It's one thing to receive the care of a friend or welcome a listening ear, but to realize that Jesus is ministering to us through these relationships, that he is entering into the mess — cleaning out the toe jam, so to speak — motivates us to put the towel over our arm, stoop over the basin, and begin washing the feet of others.

Embracing relationships in the process of spiritual growth and transformation isn't just about you; it's about God working in you and through you. Across coffee tables in living rooms, after-hours in the office, in minivans and Porsches, in back alleys, in classrooms and dorm rooms — will you let Jesus, through his people, wash your feet? And will you do the same for others?

> When he had finished washing their feet, he put on his clothes and returned to his place. "Do you understand what I have done for you?" he asked them. "You call me 'Teacher' and

'Lord,' and rightly so, for that is what I am. Now that I, your Lord and Teacher, have washed your feet, you also should wash one another's feet. I have set you an example that you should do as I have done for you. Very truly I tell you, no servant is greater than his master, nor is a messenger greater than the one who sent him. Now that you know these things, you will be blessed if you do them."

— John 13:12–17

As Jesus says, now that we know these things, we will be blessed *if we do them*. Blessing is not an arbitrary act of God; it is something that naturally accompanies a life of service to others. Blessings come when we actually care, when we stoop down to serve others in love. Your church is called to be part of this, but it will mean getting your hands dirty.

You'll have to first give a flying rip. You'll need to open up your heart to love, to risk, to fail, and you'll need to let God change you.

The question is — will you?

AFTERWORD
CAUSE A STIR!

Several months ago, I made a decision that shocked my family and friends—and will likely shock you as well, if you remember what I shared about my dislike for running. I entered, trained for, and ran a 5K race. Why in the world would I—someone who despises running—actually sign up to run a race?

Truth be told, one of the reasons I ran was that the race "swag" involved a personal vat of warm, melty, messy chocolate fondue and a steaming mug of hot chocolate. It was delicious! But that's only part of the answer—and not the main reason. I entered, trained, and ran primarily because I wanted to share the experience with a good friend. We made the journey together, training together and then running parts of the race together. We both went farther, and much faster, than we could have alone. In fact, this morning as I write this I'm wearing the sweatshirt from the race. I continue to wear it as a reminder that I need others in my life to help me stay in the race to the finish line, to commit for the long haul.

Who keeps you on track, running the race with you? Hopefully you have at least one or two close friends who can share the journey as you learn to follow Jesus together. If you don't, make this a top priority today. No one should run the race of the spiritual life alone. We all need running partners.

I hope this brief outline of the stages of formation and the suggestions for relationships at each stage of the race have increased your awareness and deepened your resolve to support spiritual growth through intentional relationships in your church community. With an increased focus on relationships, you will find greater challenges rising up — challenges that lead to even greater rewards. Practically, start watching for the signs of life I shared in several chapters, for the evidence that lives are changing and people are growing in their faith.

And remember that the work you do is *with God* to bring about what is good — his perfect will. My hope in these pages is that I've been able to identify three key concepts that can better inform the process of spiritual formation in the local church.

1. It is possible to migrate from a one-size-fits-all approach to small groups to a process that distinguishes between stages of maturity and recognizes the unique relational needs at each stage.
2. It is important to introduce spiritual practices throughout this process, but they need to be established in focused and intentional ways once a foundation has been laid and Christ followers are beginning to take increased ownership of their spiritual vitality and growth.
3. It is essential to see that mature believers aren't just useful for training up new believers. These mature followers need help to continue growing — not just through service, but through highly discerning relationships that help them stay the course and run the race to the finish line.

The local church is where the hope of the gospel is *proclaimed*. But it can also be the place where that hope is *realized* and visibly *seen*. God is at work, bringing about his good — his will — and he is doing it through transformed relationships. As the hands and feet and eyes and arms of our wounded and resurrected Savior, we are increasingly marked by his inner character and likeness.

It's time to cause a *stir* in the church and in the world.

Are you ready?

ACKNOWLEDGMENTS

"Mindy, there is nothing new under the sun; we all share the wisdom we've received from others."

— One of my mentors

I want to acknowledge those who knowingly or unknowingly have contributed to the message of *STIR*. I've been deeply blessed by mentors, work associates, friends, and family members who have filled my life, and thus these pages, with their wisdom and love, whether named or unnamed. I remain grateful for, indebted to, and forever changed by each one.

I'd like to thank Nancy Raney, who championed the message of authentic transformation, personally and professionally, from the very first time we met and over these many years since. Also, Kim Anderson and Amy Pierson faithfully researched, listened, transcribed, drafted, and otherwise helped bring together many disparate parts into one complete whole. Their fingerprints are everywhere.

Once this message was drafted, the amazing editorial team at Zondervan, including Ryan Pazdur and Dirk Buursma, made me realize afresh why authors are so indebted to their editors! They fully entered into this message and have made it much better in form and function than it would have been otherwise.

Finally, I want to acknowledge the friends who share their stories, in their own words, throughout these pages. Every one of them is in vocational ministry, and their honest, brave contributions drip with both passion and authenticity.

Together, we hope to inspire you.

APPENDIXES

APPENDIX 1
SPIRITUAL DIRECTION RESOURCES

The list of resources in this appendix is not meant to be exhaustive. Ideally, it will serve as a starting point for learning more and for taking next steps in spiritual direction.

FINDING A SPIRITUAL DIRECTOR

Whether you meet in person or via Skype, you will find that a spiritual director can be a tremendous help at any stage in the spiritual journey and particularly in the Journeying Together and Following Together stages. Many of the resources listed below also provide training for becoming a spiritual director. For more information on finding a spiritual director, check out the following:

- Evangelical Center for Spiritual Wisdom (Debbie Swindoll, executive director) provides curriculum for twelve-week studies for small groups and a directory for finding spiritual directors through its Evangelical Spiritual Directors Association (ESDA); for more information, visit www.ecswisdom.org.

- Leadership Transformations, Inc. (Steve Macchia, founder and president), offers a wide range of spiritual formation resources, including spiritual direction resources, as well as a one-year retreat-based leadership community; for more information, visit www.leadershiptransformations.org/emmaus.htm.
- Christos Center for Spiritual Formation in Lino Lakes, Minnesota, offers spiritual direction, a directory of their graduates, and a variety of retreats, workshops, and pilgrimages; for more information, visit www.christoscenter.org.
- The Transforming Center (Ruth Haley Barton, founder) offers many terrific resources for spiritual formation, including a directory of recommended spiritual directors; for more information, visit www.transformingcenter.org.
- Spiritual Directors International has a multi-faith directory of spiritual directors, including many Christians; for more information, visit www.sdiworld.org.

BECOMING A SPIRITUAL DIRECTOR

For more information on becoming a spiritual director, check out the following:

- Leadership Transformations, Inc. (Steve Macchia, founder and president), offers the Selah certificate program in spiritual direction; for more information, visit www.leadership transformations.org/selah.htm.

    The ministry also offers an excellent process for leadership teams to develop their discernment in decision making. Since many in the Following Together stage serve as leaders, these resources are particularly helpful in cultivating spiritual discernment within teams. Downloadable guides and consulting services are available; for more information, visit www. leadershiptransformations.org/sdt.htm.
- The Institute for Spiritual Formation at Talbot School of Theology and Biola University (John Coe, institute director) offers graduate programs in spiritual formation and soul care;

for more information, visit www.biola.edu/spiritualformation/ programs.

- Christos Center for Spiritual Formation, located in Lino Lakes, Minnesota, offers a two-year certificate program called "Tending the Holy," which prepares participants for the ministry of spiritual direction; for more information, visit www.christoscenter.org.
- Shalem Institute for Spiritual Formation, located near Washington, DC, offers many training opportunities; for more information, visit www.shalem.org.

APPENDIX 2
REVEAL FINDINGS

In 2007 the Willow Creek Association published the findings from research conducted on an unprecedented scale. The study has now extended to 1,600 churches, representing some 480,000 individual surveys taken in five countries. The groundbreaking REVEAL data focused on patterns that emerged when congregants were asked about their spiritual lives in the context of their church.

Here are some key findings:

1. Involvement in church activities does not predict or drive long-term spiritual growth. But there is a spiritual continuum that is very predictable and powerful.
2. Spiritual growth is all about increasing relational closeness to Christ.
3. The church is most important in the early stages of spiritual growth. Its role then shifts from being a primary influence to a secondary influence.

4. Personal spiritual practices are the building blocks for a Christ-centered life.
5. A church's most effective evangelists, volunteers, and donors come from the most spiritually advanced segments.
6. More than 25 percent of those surveyed described themselves as spiritually "stalled" or "dissatisfied" with the role of the church in their spiritual growth.
7. The need for relationships actually increases over the course of spiritual development, though the nature of the relationships changes with maturity.

For more information on REVEAL and the REVEAL Spiritual Life Survey, visit www.revealnow.com.

APPENDIX 3
TEST YOUR BIBLE IQ*

1. Who wrote the first four books of the New Testament?
2. Who wrote the first five books of the Old Testament?
3. Which two Old Testament books are named for women?
4. What is the Great Commission?
5. What is the book of Acts about?
6. Which angel appeared to Mary?
7. Who was known as the wisest man in the world?
8. Which city fell after the Israelites marched around it daily for seven days?
9. What did God give the Israelites to eat in the wilderness?
10. What was Jesus' first miracle?
11. Who was the "weeping prophet"?
12. What is the Greatest Commandment?
13. On what occasion was the Holy Spirit given to the church?

---

*For more questions, visit Probe Ministries to view the "Bible Literacy Quiz," www.probe.org/site/c.fdKEIMNsEoG/b.4221247/k.261/Bible_Literacy_Quiz.htm.

14. Who was the female judge of Israel?
15. Who was the strongest man on earth?
16. What is the last book of the Old Testament?
17. Who was the first martyr?
18. Who was Paul's first ministry partner?
19. Which event caused God to splinter human language into many tongues?
20. Who was the Hebrew who became prime minister of Egypt?
21. What is the root of all kinds of evil?
22. Who are the Major Prophets?
23. What was the Old Testament feast that celebrated God's protection of the firstborn of Israel on the night they left Egypt?
24. Which cupbearer to a foreign king rebuilt the wall of Jerusalem?
25. Which two people walked on water?

ANSWERS

1. Matthew, Mark, Luke, and John.
2. Most conservative scholars hold that the Pentateuch was written by Moses.
3. Esther and Ruth.
4. "Therefore go and make disciples of all nations, baptizing them in the name of the Father and of the Son and of the Holy Spirit, and teaching them to obey everything I have commanded you. And surely I am with you always, to the very end of the age" (Matthew 28:19–20).
5. The early years of the church, as the gospel begins to spread throughout the world.
6. Gabriel (Luke 1:26).
7. Solomon (1 Kings 3:12).
8. Jericho (Joshua 6:20).
9. Manna and quail (Exodus 16).
10. Jesus turned water into wine at the wedding at Cana (John 2:11).
11. Jeremiah.

12. "Love the Lord your God with all your heart and with all your soul and with all your mind" (Matthew 22:37).

13. Pentecost (Acts 2:1–4).

14. Deborah (Judges 4:4).

15. Samson (Judges 13–16).

16. Malachi.

17. Stephen (Acts 7).

18. Barnabas (Acts 13:2).

19. The building of the Tower of Babel (Genesis 11).

20. Joseph (Genesis 41:41).

21. The love of money (1 Timothy 6:10).

22. Isaiah, Jeremiah, Ezekiel, and Daniel.

23. Passover (Exodus 12:27).

24. Nehemiah (Nehemiah 2:5).

25. Jesus and Peter (Matthew 14:29).

APPENDIX 4
GUIDES FROM THE PAST

Those who journey through the desert are often "met" by guides in the pages of books. It's no wonder that Augustine's *Confessions*, Brother Lawrence's *The Practice of the Presence of God*, and, more recently, Thomas Kelly's *A Testament of Devotion* have stood the test of time. Thomas à Kempis wrote *The Imitation of Christ* in Latin during the years 1418–1427. Next to the Bible itself, it is the most widely published devotional book ever.

AUGUSTINE

Confessions was written sometime during AD 397 or 398 and is filled with deep meaning for us today.

> This is the fruit of my confessions of what I am, not of what I have been, to confess this, not before Thee only, in a secret exultation with trembling, and a secret sorrow with hope; but in the ears also of the believing sons of men, sharers of my joy, and partners in my

mortality, my fellow citizens, and fellow pilgrims, who are gone before, or are to follow on, companions of my way.[1]

BROTHER LAWRENCE

Brother Lawrence entered a monastery in France and lived the last thirty years of his life working in the kitchen, cooking meals and washing pots and pans. In his beloved classic, *The Practice of the Presence of God*, he writes these words:

> There is not in the world a kind of life more sweet and delightful than that of a continual conversation with God; those only can comprehend it who practice and experience it . . .
>
> I still believe that all spiritual life consists of practicing God's presence, and that anyone who practices it correctly will soon attain spiritual fulfillment.[2]

Amid the monotony of cooking and cleaning chores, Brother Lawrence's work was his ministry, rooted in his deep love for God.

> We can do little things for God; I turn the cake that is frying on the pan for love of him, and that done, if there is nothing else to call me, I prostrate myself in worship before him, who has given me grace to work; afterwards I rise happier than a king. It is enough for me to pick up but a straw from the ground for the love of God.[3]

THOMAS KELLY

Thomas Kelly was a Quaker missionary, educator, speaker, author, and scholar. In *A Testament of Devotion*, he wrote this about inward prayer:

> Live this present moment, this present hour as you now sit in your seats, in utter, utter submission and openness toward him. Listen outwardly to these words, but within, behind the scenes, in the deeper levels of your lives where you are all alone with God the Loving Eternal One, keep up a silent prayer. "Open Thou my life. Guide my thoughts where I dare not let them go. But Thou darest. Thy will be done." Walk on the streets and chat with your friends.

But every moment behind the scenes be in prayer, offering yourselves in continuous obedience.

I find this internal continuous prayer life absolutely essential. It can be carried on day and night, in the thick of business, in home and school. Such prayer of submission can be so simple. It is well to use a single sentence, repeated over and over and over again, such as this: "Be Thou my will. Be Thou my will," or "I open all before Thee. I open all before Thee," or "See earth through heaven. See earth through heaven." This hidden prayer life can pass, in time, beyond words and phrases into mere ejaculations, "My God, my God, my Holy One, my Love," or into the adoration of the Upanishad, "O Wonderful, O Wonderful, O Wonderful." Words may cease and one stands and walks and sits and lies in wordless attitudes of adoration and submission and rejoicing and exultation and glory.[4]

THOMAS À KEMPIS

Thomas à Kempis's *The Imitation of Christ* was first published in 1441. It has been called the "perfect expression of a spiritual movement known as *devotio moderna* (modern devotion), which swept Roman Catholicism through the fourteenth to sixteenth centuries. It stressed meditation and the inner life and cautioned against the outer life of much busyness and occupation."[5]

Many people try to escape temptations, only to fall more deeply. We cannot conquer simply by fleeing, but by patience and true humility we become stronger than all our enemies. The man who only shuns temptations outwardly and does not uproot them will make little progress; indeed they will quickly return, more violent than before.

Little by little, in patience and long-suffering you will overcome them, by the help of God rather than by severity and your own rash ways. Often take counsel when tempted; and do not be harsh with others who are tempted, but console them as you yourself would wish to be consoled.[6]

Whether in print or in person, fellow travelers help us interpret the unfamiliar landscape of our interior world and the activity of the Holy Spirit. They model a deep devotion to God that should inspire us to follow a similar path.

NOTES

PREFACE: A SOLITARY JOURNEY

1. To date, the REVEAL database includes survey input from approximately 480,000 congregants in 1,600 churches in 5 countries and 4 languages. For more information about REVEAL and the Spiritual Life Survey, visit www.reveal now.com.
2. Gary W. Moon and David G. Benner, *Spiritual Direction and the Care of Souls: A Guide to Christian Approaches and Practices* (Downers Grove, Ill.: InterVarsity, 2004), 11.

INTRODUCTION: ROCKET FUEL FOR THE SOUL

1. Greg L. Hawkins and Cally Parkinson, *Move: What 1,000 Churches Reveal about Spiritual Growth* (Grand Rapids: Zondervan, 2011); see especially part 2: Spiritual Movement.
2. Hawkins and Parkinson, *Move*, 120.

3. Greg L. Hawkins and Cally Parkinson, *Follow Me: What's Next for You?* (Barrington, Ill.: Willow Creek Association, 2008), 46.

CHAPTER 1: START STRONG

1. See American Bible Society, "The State of the Bible 2012," http://uncover.americanbible.org/state-bible (accessed March 1, 2013).

CHAPTER 2: BUILD THE FOUNDATION

1. Campus Crusade for Christ, the Navigators, and InterVarsity Christian Fellowship are some of the curriculum providers I'm familiar with.
2. Greg L. Hawkins and Cally Parkinson, *Move: What 1,000 Churches Reveal about Spiritual Growth* (Grand Rapids: Zondervan, 2011), 23.
3. For more on spiritual gifts, I recommend the Network material. This comprehensive resource helps people discover their spiritual gifts and empowers them for ministry. Visit www.willowcreek.com for more information.
4. David Kinnaman and Gabe Lyons, *unchristian: What a New Generation Really Thinks about Christianity ... and Why It Matters* (Grand Rapids: Baker, 2007).

CHAPTER 3: OWN THE JOURNEY

1. Sue Monk Kidd, *When the Heart Waits: Spiritual Direction for Life's Sacred Questions* (San Francisco: HarperSanFrancisco, 1992), 26.
2. See Mark 8:34. Not surprisingly, one of the most important character qualities to develop if we want to be available for God's purposes is humility, and it is one of the most difficult character qualities to be shaped in a human soul. Jesus' disciples struggled with it, just as we do. But if we are going to be shaped

into the character of Jesus, humility is required. God will only
entrust his work to those who want to do it the way God wants
it done. It certainly doesn't come naturally.

3. These six practices form a strong core of healthy individual
spiritual practices. Dozens of additional practices can be considered. These include silence, fasting, confession, submission,
worship, meditation, journaling, giving, service, and so forth.

4. Henri Nouwen, *The Inner Voice of Love: A Journey through
Anguish to Freedom* (New York: Doubleday, 1996), 109–10.

5. David Benner, *The Gift of Being Yourself: The Sacred Call to
Self Discovery* (Downers Grove, Ill.: InterVarsity, 2004), 57.

6. Gerald May, *The Dark Night of the Soul: A Psychiatrist
Explores the Connection between Darkness and Spiritual Growth*
(San Francisco: HarperSanFrancisco, 2004).

7. Ibid., 67–68.

8. Ibid.

9. Quoted in ibid., 25.

CHAPTER 4: BECOME A DESERT GUIDE

1. Heather Zempel, *Community Is Messy: The Perils and Promise
of Small Group Ministry* (Downers Grove, Ill.: InterVarsity,
2012), 24–25.

2. Mark Buchanan, *Your Church Is Too Safe: Why Following
Christ Turns the World Upside Down* (Grand Rapids: Zondervan, 2012), 131–32.

3. Parker Palmer, *A Hidden Wholeness: The Journey toward an
Undivided Life* (San Francisco: Wiley, 2008), 57–59.

4. See Laura K. Lawless, "*Savoir* vs *Connaître*: French Verbs to
Know," http://french.about.com/od/grammar/a/savoir
connaitre.htm (accessed March 1, 2013).

5. From a message by John Burke titled "re:volution: re:formation"
at Gateway Church, Austin, Texas, November 27, 2005.

6. For more information, visit www.soulcare.com and www.ivpress.com/cgi-ivpress/book.pl/code=1086 (accessed March 1, 2013).

7. For more information, visit www.ivpress.com/cgi-ivpress/book.pl/code=3540 (accessed March 1, 2013).

8. Larry Crabb, "A Brief Statement on the NewWay Understanding of Spiritual Direction and Spiritual Formation," www.newwayministries.org/ssd2.php (accessed March 1, 2013).

9. See Christ Church of Oak Brook, "Spiritual Direction," http://my.cc-ob.org/10127/content/content_id/22662/Spiritual-Direction (accessed March 1, 2013).

10. Henri Nouwen, *The Inner Voice of Love: A Journey through Anguish to Freedom* (New York: Doubleday, 1996), xiii–xiv.

CHAPTER 5: STAY THE COURSE

1. From Gary Haugen's introduction of Pranitha Timothy at the Global Leadership Summit at Willow Creek Community Church on August 10, 2012.

2. Erwin McManus, *The Barbarian Way: Unleash the Untamed Faith Within* (Nashville: Nelson, 2005), 53–54.

3. Dan Allender, *To Be Told: Know Your Story, Shape Your Future* (Colorado Springs: WaterBrook, 2005), 206.

4. Dallas Willard, *Renovation of the Heart: Putting On the Character of Christ* (Colorado Springs: NavPress, 2002), 150–52.

CHAPTER 6: RUNNING TOGETHER

1. Willow Creek Association blog, "Craig Groeschel on Investing in Your Personal Development," August 23, 2012, www.wcablog.com/2012/08/craig-groeschel-on-investing-in-your-personal-development/#more-4903 (accessed April 17, 2013).

2. Alice Fryling, *Seeking God Together: An Introduction to Group Spiritual Direction* (Downers Grove, Ill.: InterVarsity, 2009), 26–27.

3. Thomas Kelly, *A Testament of Devotion* (San Francisco: HarperSanFrancisco, 1992), 96.
4. Gateway Church, "What Is a Running Partner?" www. gatewaychurch.com/grouplife-ii/ (accessed March 1, 2013).
5. Kelly, *Testament of Devotion*, 55–56.
6. Cornelius Plantinga, *Not the Way It's Supposed to Be: A Breviary of Sin* (Grand Rapids: Eerdmans, 1995), 2.

CONCLUSION: GIVE A FLYING RIP

1. To learn more about Palm Valley's story and other best-practices churches, see Greg L. Hawkins and Cally Parkinson, *Move: What 1,000 Churches Reveal about Spiritual Growth* (Grand Rapids: Zondervan, 2011).
2. Stephen R. Covey, *The 7 Habits of Highly Effective People: Powerful Lessons in Personal Change* (New York: Fireside, 1990), 83–86; for a good summary, visit www.stephencovey. com/7habits/7habits-habit1.php (accessed March 1, 2013).

APPENDIX 4: GUIDES FROM THE PAST

1. Augustine, *Confessions*, book 10, chapter 4 (London: Dent, 1907), 207.
2. Brother Lawrence, *The Practice of the Presence of God* (Radford, Va.: Wilder, 2008), 39, 60.
3. Brother Lawrence, *The Practice of the Presence of God and the Spiritual Maxims* (Mineola, N.Y.: Dover, 2012), 61.
4. Thomas Kelly, *A Testament of Devotion* (San Francisco: HarperSanFrancisco, 1992), 33–34.
5. Richard Foster and Emilie Griffin, *Spiritual Classics: Selected Readings on the Twelve Spiritual Disciplines* (San Francisco: HarperSanFrancisco, 2000), 148.
6. Thomas à Kempis, *The Imitation of Christ* (Mineola, N.Y.: Dover, 2003), 10.

MOVE

What 1,000 Churches Reveal about Spiritual Growth

Greg L. Hawkins and Cally Parkinson, authors of Reveal

One of the church's primary responsibilities is to foster genuine spiritual growth in people's lives. Today's pastors bring tremendous effort and passion to this task, but they are often disappointed by people who sit in the pews for years, knowing about Jesus but never really knowing him.

In 2004, Willow Creek Community Church in suburban Chicago undertook a three-year study to measure spiritual growth called the REVEAL Spiritual Life Survey. Over the next six years, additional data was collected from over a quarter million people in well over a thousand churches of every size, denomination, and geographic area.

MOVE presents fact-based and somewhat startling findings from the latest REVEAL research, drawing on compelling stories from actual people—congregation members of varying spiritual maturity, as well as pastors who candidly share their disappointments and successes. It provides a new lens through which church leaders can see and measure the evidence of spiritual growth.

The local church is uniquely equipped to challenge people to pursue lives of full devotion to Christ. *MOVE* helps pastors and church leaders direct that challenge with confidence as they lead their congregations to move closer to Christ.

Available in stores and online!

SOULCARE

Practical wisdom and deeper connections on the journey to a new *way of life*

DISCOVERING SOUL CARE
MINDY CALIGUIRE

SPIRITUAL FRIENDSHIP
MINDY CALIGUIRE

SOUL SEARCHING
MINDY CALIGUIRE

SIMPLICITY
MINDY CALIGUIRE

Check out the Soul Care Resources online at www.soulcare.com